THE
sixty
MINUTE
MOTHER

talks to
Rob Parsons

Hodder & Stoughton
LONDON SYDNEY AUCKLAND

British Library Cataloguing in Publication Data
A record for this book is available from the British Library

ISBN 0 340 63061 2

Typeset by Avon Dataset Ltd, Bidford-on-Avon, Warks

Printed and bound in Great Britain by
Clays Ltd, St Ives plc

Hodder & Stoughton Ltd
A Division of Hodder Headline
338 Euston Road
London NW1 3BH

To Lyndon and Celia Bowring

for the years of wisdom, encouragement
and friendship – thank you.

Who ran to help me when I fell,
And would some pretty story tell,
Or kiss the place to make it well?
My mother.

Anne Taylor, *Original Poems*[1]

A mother is neither cocky
nor proud because she knows that the school
headmaster may call at any minute to report that
her child has just driven a motorcycle through
the school gymnasium.

Mary Kay Blakely

Contents

Acknowledgments   xi

Chapter 1   A Man on Motherhood   1
Chapter 2   When a Mother Remembers   7
    – Dianne Parsons
    Sixty Second Wisdom   14
    Take a Break   15
Chapter 3   When a Mother Accepts   19
    Sixty Second Wisdom   35
    Take a Break   36
Chapter 4   When a Mother Is Asked 'Do You   40
    Work?'
    Sixty Second Wisdom   57
    Take a Break   58
Chapter 5   When a Mother Is Alone   62
    Sixty Second Wisdom   72
    Take a Break   73
Chapter 6   When a Mother Is Sick   80
    – Wendy Bray
Chapter 7   When a Mother Feels Guilty   83
    Sixty Second Wisdom   101
    Take a Break   102
Chapter 8   When a Mother Lets Go   107

Notes   114

Acknowledgments

Wendy Bray and Jill Worth have been with me on this project since the beginning. They have advised me, guided me, helped me gather material from other mothers and written some of the 'Take a Breaks'. Jill is a single-parent mum of Sophie aged fifteen and Thomas aged eight. Wendy is married to Richard and has two children, Lois aged thirteen and Benjamin aged ten. As I write, she is in the middle of intensive chemotherapy and shares something of her story in the chapter, 'When a Mother Is Sick'. My wife Dianne has lived this book with me since she started to open our home to women, most of them mothers, over ten years ago. I would not have attempted this book without the ongoing counsel of these three women.

Sheron Rice, my assistant, has shown commitment to this project and patience beyond the call of duty. That was no surprise to me; Sheron has recently lost her own mother and could not have had a better mother or loved her more. Her contribution to this book was literally a labour of love dedicated on behalf of her and her sister Joy to the memory of their mum.

Thank you also to Lisa Curtis, Tom Beardshaw, Celia Bowring, Lyndon Bowring, Caroline Adams, Kate Hancock, Gill Williams and Steve Williams. Jonathan

Booth has played his normal role of sergeant-major and therapist.

Judith Longman, Charles Nettleton and the team at Hodder & Stoughton have been brilliant as ever – supportive, encouraging and patient!

And, above all, gratitude to the mothers who contributed. To protect privacy I've sometimes changed your names, but not your stories.

Chapter 1
A Man on Motherhood

Shortly after I wrote *The Sixty Minute Father* two things began to happen. First, mothers began to write to me saying how much they enjoyed it and that really it was a book for them as well. Second, all the research we were able to do showed us it was *mothers* who were mainly buying it and leaving it around for the men in their lives to read!

Over the past twelve years over two hundred thousand people have attended the family seminars at which I speak. The vast proportion of these are mothers. In the intervals and coffee breaks it is invariably mothers who wait to speak with me; this is true whether we are in Paris, Moscow, Vancouver or Manchester. Every year tens of thousands of people contact us in relation to our work with families; the majority of them are mothers. Much of our work has been with lone parents – for the past five years we have organised holidays specifically for lone parents and their families – and again most are mothers.

I have listened to mums who feel they have blown it irretrievably; to 'stay-at-home' mums who wonder whether people think they have taken a soft option; and to 'working mums' who are struggling with a demanding toddler and an even more demanding boss – both of them have learnt how to stamp their feet when they don't get what they want. I have listened to mums who think they are the only ones whose baby won't sleep at night, and to mothers of teenagers who feel they are the only parents in the world whose child sits next to them for the whole school journey without saying a word.

I completely understand that even all this experience doesn't get me *near* being qualified to write on motherhood, but I do feel I have been in a very privileged position. Thousands of mothers have written to me, often spoken with me, and told me of lessons they have learnt. Many have said, 'I wish someone had told me about some of this when my kids were small, but I learnt it the hard way.' In *The Sixty Minute Mother* I wanted to pass on some of what those mums have told me – lessons in the art of motherhood.

Every so often, you'll see a 'Take a Break'. This is a chance to put the coffee on and just relax as all kinds of mums share what they have learnt over the years and, just as important, *how they feel*. And then, once in a while there is a 'Sixty Second Wisdom' page from mothers who have seen it all, done it all.

Almost every mother I have ever met acknowledges motherhood as a joyful, painful, exciting, mind-numbing business, and above all, as a long-haul affair. No matter how old our children are it seems the task of parenthood never ends. Fifteen years ago a mother who was ninety-five years old came into my office. She said to me, 'I can rest in peace now, my boy.' I said, 'Oh, why is that?' She replied, 'Because I've just managed to get my youngest son into an old people's home.' It turned out that he was seventy-two and a bit shaky. But she was in full control of all her faculties and having got him started in school, university and marriage, was now tying up the last few ends – *as a mother.*

'Sometimes I don't like my kids!'

Sometime over the next few days, go to your child's bedroom and take the dog-eared copy of 'Children's Best-Loved Stories' off the bookshelf. Now turn to 'The Emperor's New Clothes', put the coffee on and read. When you get to the part where the small boy yells 'The King is naked!', imbibe the honesty, let it seep into your very soul, set your coffee down and run into the streets yelling, 'Being a mother is hard!' 'Sometimes I don't like my kids!' 'Sometimes I wish I hadn't had my kids.' And as you shout, turn around, for you will see behind you thousands of mothers joining in the procession and all of them with a look of utter joy on their faces, not for the fact that they have found solutions, but for the sheer wonder that at long last the truth is out.

It was Bill Cosby who said, 'I guess the real reason that my wife and I had children is the same reason that Napoleon had for invading Russia: it seemed like a good idea at the time. Since then, however, I've had some doubts, primarily about my intelligence.'

I often meet mothers who feel that way. They are, simply, discouraged. And they are tired: tired of worrying, tired of getting the blame for all the ills in their kids' lives – from verrucas to failed examinations – and tired of feeling guilty. Occasionally a mum will confide the heart-rending realisation that she wishes she had never had children to begin with. She carries this thought like a scar for it is mingled with unbelievable love for her child.

One mother put it like this:

> *My life took on the feeling of a monotonous routine, made even more difficult with the baby's bouts of colic. They seemed to occur every night between eleven and three in the morning. One long night as I paced the floor trying to calm my screaming baby, uncontrollable tears started to flow down my face. I was slowly hit with the realisation that the fun and games were ended and we weren't playing house any more. The reality hit me with a stunning blow.*

It can be so very hard coming to terms with all of this. Society keeps telling us that parenthood is the ultimate privilege, but why then do parents often feel what appears to be sheer misery? The answer is not that we are failures, simply that we are feeling the effect of complete responsibility for the life of another person, over whom we have no final control, and who seems only intermittently either to want our involvement or be in the least grateful for it.

I have several hopes for this book. I want us to laugh together and I want all kinds of mothers to yell out, 'Thank goodness this is not just me.' I want single-parent mums to feel encouraged and not marginalised. I want mums who feel failures to be inspired not to give up. And, above all, I want mothers to feel honoured and respected. It was Gerald Ford, previous president of the

USA, who said, 'You can hold high office, but when your time is over the world will forget you.' That is not true of motherhood – your kids will remember you for ever.

I have spoken with thousands of mothers but I have only had the opportunity to observe two at close quarters . . .

The first is now ninety years old. My abiding memory is of her clearing tables in the restaurant of a large store, so she could get enough money together by Christmas to buy me the chemistry set that sat proudly on the shelf in the toy department. She had no formal education to speak of, but she possessed a wisdom that seemed at times almost from another world. If she had any fault it was probably that she loved her children too much – to the exclusion of all else. I have always feared the day she would die, but, in truth, I have got used to losing my mother. About three years ago her mind began to become very confused. I went to visit one day and she said, 'How are you, son?' 'Oh,' I replied, 'not bad – I'm a bit worried about the kids.' I waited for her normal wisdom, but instead she looked up and said, 'I'm having my hair done today.' And suddenly she was gone – oh, still present, but lost to me. I have grieved for her over three years. She is a wonderful mother.

The second, of course, is my wife Dianne. We have been married for almost thirty years. She is an unusual mother; she had to be. Dianne has not only cared for our children, Katie and Lloyd, but for Ron who is four years older than us. He spent most of his young life in the care of the local authority and we knew him when we were in our teens. He was pretty well homeless when he knocked on our door one night near Christmas. Dianne asked him to stay the night with us. That was twenty-five years ago and he has never left. He has been with us longer than the kids. She jokes that she practised on Ron and it gave her a head start. Dianne is one of the most honest people I know, and I thought a wonderful way to start our time together would be to ask an honest mother to share some memories . . .

Chapter 2
When a Mother Remembers
– *Dianne Parsons*

I often have to drive past the infants' school that my children attended. My daughter Katie is now twenty-two, my son Lloyd, nineteen, and yet I only have to glance at the gates at the end of the playground for a million memories to come flooding back. Suddenly it is a crisp September morning and it is my daughter's first day at school. We walk from our home together, her hand tightly gripping mine. The excitement and bravado of this step into the world of the 'big children' seem to desert her the moment we close the front door, and now she looks white and worried and I catch her nibbling her bottom lip – a sure sign that tears are close at hand.

I edge her down the road towards the school and talk of anything except this special day. She mumbles replies but I catch her watching the other children to whom this is all old-hat; the kids who jostle us are seven-year-old veterans. She begins to slow her step and I begin to fear the worst when suddenly an angel appears, or so it seems to me. Actually it is her best friend for whom this is also the first day. Suddenly Katie leaves my side and runs towards Rhian. I am left standing watching as these two little girls walk solemnly up the school drive together, holding hands and each clutching a 'My Little Pony' lunch-box. I feel my eyes fill up and then Katie turns and shouts, 'See you later, Mum!'

Against all the predictions my shy, careful child has done it. She has begun.

And then my mind fast forwards three years. It is Lloyd's first day. The parenting gurus tell us that if your first child is shy, careful and compliant your second will be different. Lloyd was desperate not to disappoint those experts. In fact, he has dedicated most of his young life to proving them correct in every detail. I knew that his first day of school would be quite different – I just didn't have any idea how different.

In an event never to be repeated he was up and dressed before me and hammering on my bedroom door yelling, 'Come on, I want to get there early!' As I had with Katie, I took his hand as we walked down the road together, but whereas Katie had found this comforting, Lloyd looked as though somebody had tethered him to a walking embarrassment. He dragged me towards the place of learning, firing off threatening glances at children twice his size, and, with a burst of impatience, finally broke loose and ran ahead. I turned a corner and saw he was almost at the gate. And then it happened. He took one look into the playground, grimaced at a teacher, and then slowly walked back to me and said, 'I'm not going.'

I immediately clicked into my 'No-pain-no-gain', 'You'll-be-sorry-when-you're-thirty' and 'Superman-went-to-school' routine. He looked up with that little jaw set in the now familiar look of defiance and repeated,

'I'm not going.' And so the battle began. There were moments over the following ten minutes when it seemed possible that with the aid of other mothers I would loosen his grip on the lamp post. But he held firm. The prospect of Lloyd beginning his formal education linked to twenty feet of vertical concrete with a light on top was rushing through my brain when the deputy head appeared.

I have never managed to work out whether her concern was for me, Lloyd or the property of the county council, but she ordered me to leave. I will never forget Lloyd's face. He was torn between running after me – which meant giving up his hold on the lamp post – or remaining within the influence of a woman who looked decidedly less sympathetic to the plight of small boys than his mother. He hesitated and I went – not willingly, but propelled along by Sheila Harrison who had done all this four times already. As she whisked me away she said, 'He'll be better off without you.' I have since wondered whether she meant just at that moment or in life generally.

But on that morning, at least, she was right and I had finally ushered my two children into the 'real' world. How was I to know that motherhood involves a million school gate experiences at every age and that the process was only just starting? Why didn't somebody tell me? I'll tell you the reason – because if they had, you'd have never got *me* off that lamp post!

The Way We Were

As I look back on my kids' lives so many recollections come flooding back.

Every time early September comes, with the first hint of autumn crispness, I am immediately transported to the maternity ward and Katie's birth. I remember lying there, having gone in early with high blood pressure, and wondering what motherhood was going to be like.

And I remember another autumn morning just after Lloyd was born. Katie was a toddler and my new son was asleep in the room next to me. It was about seven in the morning and the sun was streaming through the curtains. It was in so many ways a perfect day. I had two children, a lovely home and a good husband. But none of that seemed to be very real at that moment and I turned, woke Rob, and said, 'I don't think I can cope any more. Will you take Katie to nursery today?'

Those words ushered in some dark years for Rob and me. I've no doubt that what they call post-natal depression was part of it, but the medics also found a problem with my immune system. Some days I would just lie in bed. Most friends were kind, others had advice on how to 'snap out of it' and reminded me that there were those who were a lot worse off than me. The strange thing is that the main emotion I felt was not sadness or worry, but guilt. Why couldn't I cope? What would all this do to my children? Why wasn't I a better mother?

I would love to put my arms around young mothers going through similar experiences and tell them that they can come through these dark times. I would love to explain to partners what is going on, and urge them to both care and patience. I now have the opportunity to speak to thousands of women through our seminar programme and perhaps it's as well that autumn morning is still fresh in my mind. It has left me vulnerable and therefore, I think, understanding.

I feel that illness robbed me of quite a lot of Lloyd's young life but I still have some wonderful memories: one is of him giggling. He had such an infectious giggle; sometimes I would be so angry with him, but against all my will he'd make me laugh.

I remember the joy of him when he was so very tactile; even up until he was twelve he would lie with me on the settee and put his arm in mine. And I remember the feeling almost of grief in his teenage years when that suddenly stopped and it appeared he didn't want to be seen out with me unless I had a brown paper bag over my head. And I remember when in later teens I saw the first signs of a thaw after such a long winter and how it warmed my heart.

I remember Lloyd telling me he would never marry anybody else except me, and both my kids telling me when they were young that they would never leave home. And I remember, when they were teenagers, worrying in case they meant it.

I remember being a little overweight (what do I mean 'remember' – I *am* a little overweight!) and Katie asking me to go shopping with her – that's 'size eight' Katie. We both took clothes into the changing rooms. I nearly brought the wall of the cubicle down losing my balance trying to get into a skirt I should have known was a size too small. And then when I was at my lowest, red faced and depressed, the curtain went back and Katie stood there looking absolutely stunning in a little black number and said, 'Does my bottom look big in this?' I wanted to attack her.

I remember being jealous if they went through times when they communicated with Rob more than me. I remember being desperately hurt if they didn't want to eat the meals I'd prepared. And I remember that no matter what they had done to me during the day, and no matter how old they were, it was impossible not to feel tremendous love for them when they were asleep.

And I remember times of helpless laughter. The other day I got my little family around me and said, 'I have some important information to impart – listen well.' Rob said, 'Does this include me?' I said, 'Especially you.' Without pausing for breath I went on, 'It appears that there are some things in this house that only I can do. In case I get hit by a bus I want to pass on the wisdom of the years to you.' They stood there open mouthed.

'Today's lesson is how to replace a used toilet roll. The first part is to notice the empty roll on the holder. Unless you remove it, it will not self-destruct. Push the spindle gently and remove the empty roll. Put it in the bin, *not* on the window sill – we've stopped collecting them to make *Blue Peter* castles. Now, here's the really hard part: push the spindle again and put a new roll on. There! Now you can try it on your own next time.'

I am a mother. I am not a perfect mother – I learnt a long time ago that 'perfect' is too great a burden to carry. Nor am I 'just' a mother. I am a woman with gifts, hopes and desires that are unconnected to my two kids. But, without doubt, it is in the realm of motherhood that you will find my greatest laughter and my deepest sorrow; it is there you will discover my greatest pride and haunting fears.

Sixty Second Wisdom

(from mothers who've seen it all, done it all, worn the tee-shirt ... and survived!)

60 Guilt is an occupational hazard; learn to live with it – it comes with the placenta.

60 Ignore the dust occasionally; or, better still, teach them how to spell in it!

60 Don't be too upset when your kids don't want the meal you made. I know it doesn't help when your son comes home and says,'Tom's mum did us egg on toast.' You say, 'But you don't like eggs!', and he replies, 'I do now.' It *is* hurtful, but it's not personal.

60 Two-year-olds are not fooled by designs of a clown with a mashed potato face, a sausage nose, pea eyes, a carrot smile and broccoli hair. They *know* what broccoli is.

You're not the only mother who ...

- Says as she cleans out the rabbit, hamster and budgie cages, 'Why do I fall for it time and time again?'

- Thinks she's on a game show, where the prize goes to the mother who can find most dirty dishes in the shortest time, including those in her teenager's wardrobe.

- Honestly believes that if she were introduced to the Prime Minister, he would say, 'Nice to see you, Mrs Harries. You haven't seen my Game Boy anywhere have you?'

- Turns her daughter's dirty white socks inside out so they look clean for Brownies.

- Stays up all night making a dozen flapjacks for the school fair cake stall and then doesn't produce them on seeing that Danielle Thomas' mother has made a novelty cake in the shape of a tree-house complete with squirrel. You go straight home and eat all the flapjacks.

The First Child

I felt as though I had been in labour for most of my life, but really it was only seven hours before I heard a cry from my newborn baby daughter. Elated and relieved at the safe arrival of our much-wanted first child, my husband Michael and I wept as we held the baby together.

But two hours later, in the hospital ward, my elation gave way to panic. Gazing at my daughter through the clear sides of the cot, I was overwhelmed by the responsibility of having my own child. I thought: 'This is it now – there's no going back. She's mine for the rest of my life.'

My baby opened her eyes, and we stared at each other. I was the one to blink first. 'What have I done?' I thought. 'And where is the joy and happiness everyone told me I'd be feeling? What's wrong with me – aren't I a normal mother?'

Alison, mother of Rebecca

Nursery School

My child's nursery school has in it a box which contains spare pants for children who haven't quite mastered the art of getting to the loo on time. The other day, Emma, my three-year-old, wore a pair home. I washed them and gave them to my husband to return to the nursery when he dropped her off the next day. He was sitting on the bus with Emma when a helper from the nursery got on, smiled at them and sat down at the back. A few minutes passed and then Emma stood up, turned around and, to the amusement of the crowded bus, said, 'It's all right Miss Deverold, my father's got your knickers in his pocket.'

Chapter 3
When a Mother Accepts

'What is the greatest gift a mother can give a child?' That was the question asked of four hundred women at a recent seminar. The most common reply by a long way, was 'love'.

I'm not at all sure it is the right answer. If it is, then we should be pleased, for although most of us have critics, enemies, and those who find us just plain irritating, our mothers love us. One of the most embarrassing moments of my life occurred at 10.30 on a winter's morning when I was thirty-nine years old. At that time I was a senior partner in a legal practice and had a rather pompous and crusty bank manager as a passenger in my car. As we made our way along a busy street I saw my mother shopping. She would have been almost eighty then and was struggling with a large bag in the rain. 'That's my mother over there', I said to my passenger. 'We're very near her home; is it all right if we give her a lift?' For the first time that week the bank manager said 'Yes'.

My dear old mother clambered into the back seat and we began to make our way to the street where she lived. A few moments passed in silence and then she leant forward, tapped the banker on the shoulder, pointed at me, and said to him, 'Don't you think he's lovely?' He replied, 'Very nice indeed, Mrs Parsons.'

So if it is not love that is the greatest gift, what can it possibly be? I am convinced it is – acceptance. If a child does not feel accepted by his or her mother, it is almost impossible for them to feel loved by her.

We hear a great deal these days about 'peer pressure' with regard to raising children and it is true that this dwarfs the power of parental influence for many children, especially in the teenage years. But, in truth, peer pressure is a phenomenon that affects us all – we crave to be accepted. What else could make millions of us eat rabbit food, and torture ourselves on treadmills, or have plastic surgeons yank, stretch and redistribute vast areas of our skin so that we look younger? Somebody has convinced us that youth and a certain style of beauty are the things that make us acceptable, and what we want, almost as much as life itself, is to be accepted.

One of the greatest services we can do for our children is to send them into adulthood believing that at least their parents accept them for who they are. In the next section we look at two ways in which children perceive whether or not they really are loved like that.

'I Accept the Way You Look'

One of the greatest pressures on children in modern society is the way they look. Amongst the most rampant diseases plaguing the young are the eating disorders of anorexia and bulimia. In one study two thousand girls from eleven to eighteen were asked, 'What would you most like to change about yourself if you could?' Fifty-nine per cent mentioned some aspect of their physical appearance, with only four per cent desiring greater ability. In another study, children were asked to complete the sentence, 'I wish I were . . .'. The majority of boys answered, 'Taller' and the girls, 'Smaller'.

We live in a world in which thin is beautiful. In the western world we forget this is a purely cultural phenomenon. A friend of mine went to Uganda. On showing some of the women a photograph of her family one of them said, 'Oh, your mother is beautiful – she is fat just like you.' If you've got a moment, browse through a local art gallery. Observe the paintings of women of a few hundred years ago; I guarantee there won't be a size fourteen in sight, never mind a size ten. These were large women – and thought of as beautiful. One woman put it well: 'Society always wants women to be the shape it's hardest for us to achieve. In Victorian times when good food was hard to come by, the fashionable shape was "well-rounded". Now, with an abundance of foods, not to mention Mars bars, they want us to look like stick-insects.'

Kids aren't stupid; they know that ugly girls don't get on the front covers of teen magazines or unattractive boys adorn the inside pages. But way before that they have been introduced to the world of 'beautiful baby' competitions. One of the saddest sights imaginable must be that of adults who should know better, solemnly gazing into pram after pram and judging who is or who is not a 'beautiful baby'. What, for goodness sake, does a beautiful baby look like? And because of that pressure countless mothers who will give birth today will, over

21

the coming weeks, feel disappointed with the way their baby looks. They wanted a cuddly, rounded, rosy-cheeked, smiling, angel. What they got looks like a cross between a drowned rat and a prune.

But here's the rub: as that baby grows she will assess from a million messages – some screamed at her from adverts, some whispered in school playgrounds and most unsaid – whether or not she is 'beautiful'. Unless that child is destined to be one of the few who meet the standard she will have to do battle with the world if she is to hold on to her self-esteem. She ought not to have to do battle in the home.

Not far from us lives a very attractive mum. This woman is slim, and looks ten years younger than her forty years. Her daughter is seventeen and a little over-weight. The other day the mother, in the hearing of some of her daughter's friends, said, 'You know, Ceri, I'm forty and I'm in better shape than you.' Does that mother love her daughter? Yes, she would probably die for her. Does she accept her? No.

Who is the Fairest of Them All?

It's amazing how early in life our children imbibe the idea that they must look a certain way to be acceptable. Take, for example, some well-known children's stories. Before you switch off let me assure you, I do not think we should rewrite every fairy tale to make it politically correct. One of the funniest books published recently takes a sideways swipe at that philosophy. Here's a short example from a politically correct 'Red Riding Hood'.[2]

The wolf said, 'You know my dear, it isn't safe for a little girl to walk through these woods alone'.

Red Riding Hood said, 'I find your sexist remark offensive in the extreme, but I will ignore it because of your traditional status as an outcast from society, the stress of which has caused you to develop your own, entirely valid, world view. Now, if you'll excuse me, I must be on my way'.

Red Riding Hood walked along the main path. But, because his status outside society had freed him from slavish adherence to linear, Western-style thought, the wolf knew a quicker route to Grandma's house . . .'

But having laughed at that, just consider the role of beauty in some of these popular stories and what this may say to our kids. 'The Ugly Duckling' is a nice example. At first it looks promising – this little duckling who doesn't fit the mould and is ostracised. So how does our hero get over this? Is it by using other gifts to make his mark, or triumphing by sheer personality? No, he does it by – becoming beautiful. Inside the ugly duckling is a beautiful swan just waiting to emerge. How many kids have looked in the mirror each morning and wondered how long it will be before their swan shows up?

Or enter the world of Disney and 'Snow White and the Seven Dwarfs'. That story has a magic mirror in it. Not only does this mirror possess incredible powers, it allows you, once in a while, to ask it questions. Think of that. What question would you ask a magic mirror? Well, how about, 'Who is the fairest of them all?' We know none of the dwarfs are in the frame, but we needn't have worried, because our tall, slim, dark-haired beauty is ready to help – so long as we can stop her eating apples.

The list goes on – 'Sleeping Beauty', 'Beauty and the Beast' – but without doubt the best example is 'Cinderella'. Look at any child's illustrated book of this timeless story. In the beginning Cinderella looks dirty, unwashed, and her clothes certainly aren't designer. But there is no doubt that this woman is gorgeous. When the fairy godmother comes she doesn't give Cinders a face-lift – this kid doesn't need one – and you can bet your bottom dollar that the handsome prince wasn't bowled off his feet by the horses, or the coach, even if he did guess they were actually a bunch of mice and a pumpkin. And who, dare we ask, are the enemy? Well – the *ugly* sisters!

Am I Worth Loving?

How do we decide whether we are acceptable and have worth? The answer is that we perceive this from outside ourselves – from others – especially from those we love and respect. What makes life particularly hard is that so often when our self-esteem is at its most vulnerable, our peers are at their most hurtful. What do they sing to us on our special day when we are eight years old?

> *Happy Birthday to you.*
> *You belong in a zoo.*
> *Your face is like a monkey's.*
> *Happy Birthday to you.*

I doubt we'll ever be able to do much to change the cruelty of the very young, but life should be different around our parents. I am saddened when I hear parents make derogatory comments, even in a humorous vein, about the physical appearance of their children – especially in front of others.

The other day, Dianne complimented a teenager on her new outfit; she smiled but her mother poked a finger at a tummy that was protruding and said, 'It'll look even better when she does something about that.' Of course a parent will want to help a child who is seriously over-weight, or counsel a teenager about what he or she can do about that zit on the end of their nose, but somehow we have to let our kids know that we love them anyway. That involves us being manifestly proud of them when they are at their gawkiest, most awkward, and especially if their particular features don't happen to fit what society at present calls 'attractive'. It is so hard for us to get out of the mould. The other day there was a picture in a newspaper of a young girl who had tragically lost her life. I heard a mum standing next to me say, 'Isn't it tragic – and she was so pretty.' I understand what she meant. But it wasn't any more tragic because she was pretty. It was just tragic.

The truth is that the matter of acceptance is not just relevant to the child who does not seem very phy-sically attractive. It is probably even more important for the child who seems the epitome of all that society calls beautiful. This girl will go through her life always won-dering whether her friends, employers, and the men who say they love her, actually just want her for her looks. That child, as well as her plainer friend, desperately needs to know that her mother and father love her for who she is. It will not only enrich her childhood, but it will come in handy for that day some years down the road when she asks the question of the mirror and it says, 'Sorry, honey – not you.'

But what of the other issue by which children decide whether or not their mother really does accept them?

'I Accept You Irrespective of What You Achieve'

The second way that we show our children whether or not they are accepted is by our attitude to their achievements. One of the most testing aspects of parenthood is to balance motivating our children to reach their potential without instilling in them the belief that our love for them is conditional on how they perform. As I write, it is halfway through the month of August. For the vast majority of parents this time of year holds no special terrors, but if your child is sixteen or eighteen, the onset of the end of the summer contains trauma unimaginable: it is time for GCSE and A-level results.

Dianne and I have long since given up trying to prophesy the results of our children's examinations; in any event it is so much harder with Lloyd. When Katie came home from an examination we used to ask her how she had done. She would produce the question paper and meticulously take us through each section recalling the way she had answered, and occasionally confessing where she had been stumped. So when Lloyd hit exams we tried the same technique. He came home and we said, 'How did Maths go, son?' He answered, 'Fine'. This was very encouraging. 'Did you bring the paper home so we could look at it?' 'No – I lost it on the bus.' The next day came and with it another examination. At four o'clock we found ourselves asking, 'How was Geography?' The oracle again replied, 'Fine'. And again the paper had disappeared, this time apparently having been set fire to immediately on leaving the school. We asked about all ten subjects and received the adjudication 'Fine' to each one. Every parent wants to think the best of their children and so Dianne and I spent a blissful two weeks rejoicing that although Lloyd did not seem to have overtaxed himself on revision, his natural flair had obviously come to his aid.

It was not until we saw his school report, which had apparently only narrowly missed the same fate as befell the geography paper, that we both realised that the comment 'Fine' bore no relation at all to the results achieved. Lloyd had shown a degree of impartiality that would have done credit to an Old Bailey judge. The few successes and the cluster of disappointments had all received the same . . . 'Fine'.

Of course, since then, we have had the opportunity of observing him after many examinations and now understand that when he said 'Fine' it was actually not in relation to anything at all, least of all the recent test. It was rather a word that, loosely interpreted, meant, 'Here is a little something to keep you quiet until the truth gets out.'

I will never forget our going with Lloyd to get his GCSE results. We watched this young man walk across the playground and into the school as we sat in the car and waited. Dianne was, by now, crying but she wasn't sure why. And suddenly he appeared, results in hand. The comment that came next from his lips seemed strangely unfitting as he was now the proud possessor of a cluster of GCSEs, including English Language – 'I done wicked good, Mum!'

I promise you we have tried hard to motivate our children, and who knows whether we've succeeded or not. I am sure that we have got lots wrong in this whole area; it's possible to be too easy-going and not push a child hard enough, or to push too hard and pressurise them. But above all I have craved for them to understand that even in the middle of all the yelling, the blackmail and the forced study guides for breakfast, they should know for a certainty they were loved – anyway.

The pressure for our kids to achieve can begin at a very young age. This is how one young mum put it:

I really enjoy the 'Mother and Toddler' group; it's great for company and a chance to get out of the house, but sometimes I find it a pressure.

The mums are all very friendly but there seems to be a constant comparison of what progress our babies have made. It leaves me feeling inadequate if 'everyone else's baby' can sit up without leaning on the settee, or has started to crawl, or has quite clearly said 'Mummy'. Sometimes, though, my baby is the one in front, with most of the others lagging behind, and I feel proud at the achievement.

Already the other mothers are talking about the best nurseries – and even the best schools. I haven't thought that far ahead, but of course, I realise I must – otherwise all the other children will be reaching heights far above Gemma. There is a baby music and movement group starting up – I must get her name down straight away. And I must keep my ears open for any other classes that would aid Gemma's development. It doesn't do to fall behind in this world, and it's never too soon to begin.

I remember calling on a mum who had a six-month-old boy. I rang the bell and she yelled, 'Come in, the door's open.' I entered the hall, and hearing some noises coming from the kitchen, made my way there. I will never forget the sight that greeted me. Pamela was kneeling on the floor in front of Toby holding a knife about two inches from his face. She didn't turn round to greet me, just shouted over her shoulder, 'Grab a chair – I'll be with you in a moment.' I sat. She now turned her full attention back to the child, 'Toby, this is a knife – a *knife* Toby – this is a *knife*.' The child looked slightly more nonplussed than I and seemed more interested in the cat who at this time was tucking into Toby's stewed prune on the kitchen surface.

Eventually the knife was put down, and we had 'Toby, a *fork* – Toby, a *fork*'. I could see that this mother was utterly committed to working her way through a whole canteen of cutlery and said, 'Look – I'll come back later.' 'No,' she said, 'we're just about finished – it's his "learn a word" hour.'

I know it's not always wise to speak your mind in such moments but I couldn't resist it. 'What will he do with the word if he learns it? The child can't talk yet.' She gave me a sympathetic look and said, 'Sub-conscious'. I wasn't sure if she was referring to some educational principle or the look on my face, but she went on, 'It all goes into their little minds and later it will come popping out.'

Fortunately for him, Toby had a more realistic view of life than Pamela and seemed to feel no pressure at all to pop anything out apart from the normal. And it was good for him that he didn't, because in a world where achievement is everything, we can pressurise our kids to succeed and, in the process, all but rob them of their childhood.

At home I have a favourite mug; on it is a picture of a harassed mum in one of those 'family mover' vehicles which looks like a small bus. She is talking to a solitary young figure sitting next to her: 'If Simon's in Cubs, and Helen's in Brownies, and Mark's in Kung-fu, and Becky's at swimming . . . who the heck are you?'

Of course it's good to give children opportunities, and activities like piano lessons and ballet can be wonderful, so long as we don't try to put old heads on young shoulders and, in so doing, make it hard for those kids just to have fun. And when they do these things we need to lighten up a bit. The main aim should be that our kids enjoy playing the piano, learn to love ballet, not end up at the Festival Hall or starring in 'Swan Lake' in Moscow.

Sometimes we try to compensate for what we perceive to be our own failure through our children. We want them to do better than we did; we are anxious for them to have the opportunities that we missed. There's nothing wrong with any of that as long as we don't get too screwed up about it. Children quickly sense when something is important to us and they generally want to please, but not every child can win the school races, and even if they manage to, it's an awful burden to believe they've got to go on doing it. I was once attacked by an irate father who insisted that his son had beaten Lloyd in a swimming race by a millisecond. If it had been the Atlanta Olympics I might have got excited, but we were on holiday in Cornwall and it was the small hotel's *Fun Day*.

Just recently, I watched an American television programme. It was a documentary about beauty queens, except these were nine- and ten-year-olds. Mothers fussed and primped these prima-donnas who had learnt to walk, talk and ooze sex appeal before they had started their periods. Perhaps one of them will end up as Miss World. I just hope that when they do, and are surrounded by money, success and glitter, somebody will be able to explain to them where their childhood went.

We send our children into a world that will continually judge them. They will be forced to ask themselves: 'Am I clever enough?' 'Am I good with people?' 'Am I determined/flexible/focused/laid back . . . enough?' And, of course, 'Am I attractive enough?' Matching up to the demands of others is a wearisome business. But we do our children a wonderful service if we send them into that world with an unshakeable belief that there is at least one person who, irrespective of their grades, weight or athletic genius, loves them – *anyway*. It really is the greatest gift. Most of us, as adults, are still searching for somebody to love us like that.

Where do we find examples of such love? In my experience it is so often among those who parent children with special needs. These parents face the most difficult of circumstances and often with little help or understanding. The charity I work with runs residential weekends for those parents. Some time ago a couple attended who have a Down's syndrome child. The mother said to us, 'Our son is twenty-eight years old – in all those years this is the first evening we have ever had away on our own.' Those parents do not want anybody to romanticise the task they do; nevertheless, in the everyday challenges, in the bearing of the misunderstanding of others, and the knowledge that this is a lifelong commitment, they constantly demonstrate a love that accepts – *anyway*.

I recently received a quite remarkable letter from a mother. She had been told that she would never be able to conceive, but eleven years ago gave birth to a daughter. I felt I had to speak to her and had a wonderful telephone conversation: she urged me to always remember those who were the parents of disabled children, for they carry, as she put it, 'A responsibility, a love and a pain, that is hard to convey to those who have never been there.' This is her story:

> *When my daughter, Kelly, was born, I was told that she was blind, almost certainly intellectually impaired, and with severely dysfunctional internal organs.*
>
> *I will never forget holding this precious child in a shawl and, with tears running down my face, wondering what the future held for her. As I gazed down at her, she looked so vulnerable, and emotion after emotion was flooding through me. I suddenly had a compelling desire to commit my feelings to*

*paper. When she was just seven weeks old I wrote
my daughter a letter. I have kept it in a drawer since
the day I wrote it all those years ago. If you think it
would help others please use it.*

April 11, 1988

My darling Kelly,

As I write, you are seven weeks
old, a very beautiful baby, and
unspeakably precious to your father
and me. When you were born it was
wonderful to have you, a little
daughter. Now, with the news that
you are blind, we love you with an
even more tender love.

I have wept for you, Kelly,
these last days, as I've
remembered experiences that you
will never have. But I am also
deeply sure that all is well and
there is nothing to be afraid of in
the future.

God's hand is on you and he will
shape and fashion you, often
through heartache and pain, into an
exceptional woman. You are very
special to us.

Kelly, I want you to be the
best that you can be. Don't ever
settle for second best, making
your disability an excuse not to
be excellent. Be brave and full of

laughter. Listen with your ears and your heart to others, always seeking to bring healing and love to them. Be strong and unrelenting in your desire to live life to it's fullest. Many precious things will be withheld from you, but the best will always be there for you. Trust God.

My sweet child, I love you so much and I promise to be with you as you grow – in understanding, encouragement, in discipline and in tenderness.

Your mother

Elizabeth Thomas

A promise 'to be with you as you grow – in understanding, encouragement, discipline and tenderness'. No child could ask more from a mother.

Sixty Second Wisdom

60 Parenting is a long-haul business. Don't exhaust yourselves in the teenage years – who will they turn to in their forties?

60 Never miss an opportunity to read a story; the day is hurtling towards you when they'll say, 'Not tonight, thanks'.

60 Don't take all the credit; don't take all the blame.

60 Have a life apart from your kids – if you give yourself completely, they get less.

[Immediately after the birth] nothing had prepared me for the shock of that first meeting. How often, after all, do you meet someone for the first time, already knowing that you will love them passionately? Who was he? Would I like him? Would he like me? I thought him very lovely, but I could not shake off the eerie feeling that he disapproved of me – are you her, are you all?

Kate Saunders writing about her son Felix, in **Sons and Mothers**[3]

Supermum Always . . .

- has all the stuff to make the models on *Blue Peter*;

- returns library books several days early;

- redeems her supermarket coupons before the expiry date;

- irons her tea towels twice;

- has neatly plucked eyebrows;

- knows the school holiday dates;

- gets to the bottom of the ironing basket;

- washes PE kit every Friday night without fail.

Pingu, Pingu, Pingu

Yawning, I make the Pingu jigsaw with Joe for the fifth time today. We've read the Pingu book at least six times and watched the Pingu video twice. Pingu is Joe's latest craze. Meanwhile, I am so bored with Pingu that I think it possible I might scream very loudly.

I just have to get out of the house at least once today, although I haven't any shopping to do and my friends are either out at work or busy elsewhere. 'Let's go to the park', I say cheerfully to Joe. 'Want Pingu telly,' says Joe.

I struggle to get Joe into his coat and buggy, and push him, protesting, to the nearest park. Once he gets there, of course, he loves every minute. But after his sixth go on the swing and the twelfth turn on the slide, I am so bored with the park that I think it possible I might scream very loudly... *indeed*!

I love Joe so much. I really do. It's just that after having a fulfilling career, I'm finding full-time motherhood tedious, and it makes me feel so *guilty*.

Gillian, mother of Joe

Chapter 4

When a Mother Is Asked 'Do You Work?'

or

'If staying at home is so fulfilling why am I climbing the walls with boredom?'

'If working outside the home is so liberating why am I permanently shattered?'

I'm glad of the five-year gap between writing *The Sixty Minute Father* and this book on motherhood. Those years have given me time to talk to thousands of men about the scourge of over-busyness that is killing families. *The Sixty Minute Father* was written to urge men not to miss spending time with their children, and to encourage them to get involved in their lives. That book was not written out of my success but my failure. My children are now grown but when they were small I was often just too busy. I suppose the quote that best sums it up is, 'Nobody ever said on their deathbed, "I wish I'd spent more time at the office." '

Let me give you a flavour of what I have been saying to fathers:

A Father Looks Back

A father sat and flipped through a family album. His children were almost adults, and the day when the home was free of untidy bedrooms and blaring music was closer than he wanted. Not an organized album, this one: nobody had, in the suggested manner, written the date and place on the back of each photograph. Eighteen years of home life were randomly thrown together. Yet one could still read in those memories the unmistakable journey this family had made together through the years.

There was a toddler with a broad smile, who showed no hint of embarrassment that he had just one tooth. Two children played on a beach. A shepherd clung grimly to a stuffed lamb in a nativity play that even a kind critic would have described as low-budget. There were Christmases, aunts and uncles and enough animals for a small zoo.

Then the father sighed and reached for a photograph tucked into the sleeve of the album. Smiling out of the photograph was a young man. He stood in what was obviously a hospital room, and in his hands he cradled a newborn baby. This man had built up a business, sat on numerous boards and committees, and had, without a doubt, achieved what some would call success. As he gazed at the photograph, his shoulders sagged. Finally he lifted his head and whispered, 'I would trade it all today if I could roll back the years and begin again.'

Is he a bad father? Is it that he doesn't care about his children? No, in many ways he is a good father. He loves his family. He provides for them and tries to give them the very best. If you ask him what was most important – his work, his hobbies, or his family – he would answer in a moment: 'My wife, my children.' Yet he is fifty years old, his family is grown and he feels he has missed their very childhood.

I understand him so well. When he was small, my son Lloyd used to come into the bathroom in the mornings and say, 'Dad, tell me a story while you're shaving.' Lloyd asked for those stories every day. Then one day he didn't come. He didn't send me a postcard to warn me this was going to happen. He didn't even say, 'By the way, Dad, this morning is the last one.' It was simply that on a rainy winter's day at 7.00 a.m., that particular door of childhood silently closed.

Consider those eighteen years of childhood and imagine for a moment the hourglass contains not sand but days. When your child was born, the timer had 6,570 days in it. If your child is ten years old, you have 2,920 left. No amount of money, power, or prestige can increase that number.[4]

Out of Control

Since writing *The Sixty Minute Father* I am often asked to speak to companies about the challenge of balancing home and work priorities and increasingly it is mothers who approach me at the end and say something like this: 'I understand that you wrote that book for men, but you must know that these are issues that every working mother struggles with.' The truth is, I do know it; how could I not? One of the main topics raised by women in their letters to me is the incredible pressure they live under in trying to hold down a job and run a home. Millions of women feel this way because in spite of the fact that more and more fathers are getting involved, the vast proportion of the responsibility of running the home still falls on women. Some mothers express the view to me that they have been 'liberated' from the home only to discover a new prison which actually still includes all the old duties with new ones added.

One woman put it like this:

> *People say that being a mum at home is mundane and boring and I confess that often it was, but am I the only mother who sometimes thinks, 'This job is not exactly enthralling – perhaps being tied to the house was not that much worse than being tied to the shop. At least then life was only boring – now it's boring and I'm tearing my hair out.'*

The phrase that mothers often use to describe their lives is 'out of control'. In a recent seminar for business executives I began by asking them when they thought that Formula One racing drivers were under most stress. The normal answers came thick and fast – 'On the starting grid', and 'When he's overtaking'. I shook my head and the delegates went quiet for a moment and then a woman

43

in the third row said, 'When he's pulled into the pits to get refuelled and have the tyres changed.' She was right – for the simple reason that it's the very place where the drivers don't have control. They wait anxiously as others fit the wheels or perhaps lose precious seconds fumbling with the fuel line, and finally they roar off to join the fray again.

I could see that large sections of the audience suddenly had a tremendous empathy with the lot of racing drivers. One woman said:

> *Tell me about it. I have three kids. This morning before 7.00 I had searched for homework done the previous night by my ten-year-old, done the homework for my twelve-year-old, and mopped up where the dog had been sick. The child-minder for my toddler was meant to be at the house at 7.30 a.m. Just as I was about to leave, her mother rang to say her daughter had a bad cold and wouldn't be able to come. It was all I could do to stop myself screaming down the phone, 'Bad cold! I'm here about to have a double coronary and her nose is sniffling?' As long as everything goes according to plan, life is tolerable. But so often it doesn't, and then I lose it.*

Enter . . . Supermum!

There is little worse than feeling that life is just out of control. And the problem is that so often society gives us the message that we should be able to cope – easily. Apart from single mothers, who are so often told their children are destined for disaster, working mums are the greatest recipients of guilt in the modern world. And that guilt has two aspects. First there's the worry that they and their kids are missing out because they are not at home, but a little more insidious is the nagging feeling that they should be coping much better with it all. One mum put it like this: 'Sometimes I ask myself, "Am I the only mother who gets home at teatime fully intending to cook a decent meal and who ends up bunging a frozen pizza in the oven? Do other mothers who work all day actually fall asleep telling bedtime stories, and find themselves sewing name tags onto gym kit at midnight?" '

And then, just when we thought that life couldn't get any worse, we meet *Supermum*. Supermum not only looks good – she doesn't have lipstick on her teeth, and her skirt is not tucked into the back of her tights – but she balances a demanding job and running the home with clinical efficiency. She really does seem to be able to do it all. This creature is never diverted from her game-plan. She bakes, chairs boardroom discussions and gets to every parent–teacher evening. Her kids never eat pizza for tea, and she not only doesn't fall asleep reading bedtime stories, in her spare time she writes them!

The truth is that she's probably not Supermum and in her quieter moments knows it. Anyway, who defined a successful mum as being the cleverest person at time-management or planning? Some of the best mums I know are the most chaotic – their homes, their hair and their priorities seem a mess. But their kids love them and, so it seems, do all the other kids in the neighbourhood.

It's certainly true that mothers have more freedom to

work outside the home and yet many feel trapped by doing so. When I speak to women about this issue they often raise the need for fathers to be more involved in helping in the home, and for employers to become more aware of the needs of employees who have children, but almost all agree that it's much deeper than that.

In the following pages we look at two myths that make it hard for mothers to consider these issues dispassionately. One myth demeans the role of the mother at home, and the other, the task of the mother trying to balance dual responsibilities.

Myth Number One: Looking after Children at Home Is Not a 'Proper Job'

One of the most crucial tasks facing us in a modern society and one to which individuals, the media and especially government needs to pay heed, is that of creating a climate where the task of raising children is seen as a vital and high calling. We must stop degrading the task of bringing up children and, in so doing, making the mother who decides to work part-time, stay at home while her kids are small, or stay at home completely, feel that her brain must have dropped out.

The truth is that some mums whose brains have definitely not dropped out are taking the decision to cut back their professional lives in order to spend more time with their families. Julie Akhurt, who resigned the editorship of *Best* for family reasons, said: 'The most common reaction I get is, "How can you give all this up?" which seems to imply that choosing to be a mother is not what you do if you are clever. But I have always known that is what I would do.'

Whenever I speak to mothers in our seminars, I find that whether they are mums who work outside the home or mums who stay home looking after small children, nothing gets such a strong reaction as when I relate the reply given by a mum some years ago to the question, 'Do you work?' For those of you who have heard it before, forgive me, but here's the whole context of that memorable answer.

I remember the evening so well. My husband had been invited to a business dinner and partners had the privilege of attending as well. For a good week before, I began panicking. My first son was thirteen, my daughter was three and my second son had just been born – and judging by my stomach large parts of him were still inside. I lay awake at night imagining the other women who would be there. The problem with panic is that it feeds off itself. Most parties I have attended have one woman who looks as if she's stepped off the front cover of Vogue, *but generally the rest of us are an assortment of bodies all trying to make the best of ourselves and not sure if we've managed it. But as I lay awake at night my mind began to drift and suddenly all the women in this party were leggy creatures who looked at home on a catwalk – except for one, who looked like a feature shot from* Wrestling Weekly. *One night I actually slipped out of bed without waking my husband and took a dress downstairs to see if I could get into it. The zip broke.*

The big moment eventually came and, for some reason, as I entered the room I felt quite confident. Even the sight of two other women in the same 'Wallis' shop dress only threw me slightly and I caught myself smiling at the sight of the three of us scurrying to different corners of the room. As I passed a mirror, I shot a look at myself; it may have been the lighting but I thought I looked pretty good. This wasn't going to be so bad after all. And then out of a clear blue sky came a double whammy.

The first of these said whammys came in the guise of a lovely lady whom I hadn't seen for ages. She did not intend to hurt me – she is down-to-earth, warm and caring; she was genuinely pleased to see me and came rushing across. 'What a lovely surprise – when's the baby due?' 'He's five weeks old,' I said. Bless her heart, I thought we'd have to call the paramedics – for both of us!

But it wasn't the worst moment; that came during the meal. I was sitting opposite a very attractive young female executive who, after some small talk, leant forward and asked, 'Do you work?'

It's amazing how fast the brain operates. 'Do I work?' I thought. Well, I knew that the task of motherhood made just about every other job I'd done look easy; I knew that I got up early and went to bed late; and I was sure that three young lives were utterly dependent on me. But did I work? I mumbled, 'No. I'm just a mum – at home with young children.'

Some years later I related my experience to an older mother who said, 'When somebody asks you

that again, this is what you must say . . .' I went
home and practised it, and five months later, as I
stood in a crowded room with a piece of cheese on
the end of a stick, some poor soul asked me again,
'Do you work, Karen?'

'Yes,' I replied. 'I'm in a programme of social
development. At present I'm working with three age
groups. First, with babies and toddlers. That in-
volves a basic grasp of medicine and child psycho-
logy. Next, I'm working with teenagers. I confess
the programme is not going too well in that area.
Finally, at evenings and weekends I work with a
man aged thirty-nine who's exhibiting all the classic
symptoms of mid-life crisis. That's mainly psychi-
atric work. The whole job involves planning, a "make
it happen" attitude and the ability to crisis-manage.
I used to be an international fashion model – but I
got bored.'

Yes!!!

Myth Number Two:
Balancing Home and Work Is Just
a Matter of Organisation

The heart of this delusion is that any mother worth her
salt should be able to cope with raising small children,
doing a full-time job, cooking their meals, washing their
clothes, doing their homework, reading them stories, and
still have enough energy left to be a sexual athlete. One
mother put it like this: 'If all this is so easy, why aren't
men doing it? He wants me to do all this stuff and still be
what he calls "great in bed". I said to him, "I'm exhausted.

You know when I'm great in bed? When I'm asleep." '

Many mothers feel pressured when they read that 'You can have it all' – a busy career, a fulfilling family life, and lots of social life as well. But the problem is that no matter how many time-management courses we attend and no matter how many filofax diaries we possess, the one thing we can't change is the amount of time we each have. Every day comes to us full of 86,400 seconds. It doesn't much matter whether we're the managing director of ICI or the office junior, we get the same; every day we spend it all and start the next day with another 86,400 seconds. And that means we have to choose. An old Eastern proverb says, 'If you do this – you can't do that.'

But sometimes we slip into a lifestyle in which we try to 'do it all'. A mum said to me recently:

> *I was just driving myself into the ground. John and I were like ships passing in the night and the things that should have been bringing me pleasure, like my son's football matches after school, were just an added pressure. One night we sat down and talked about it. We decided I would reduce my hours to be there when the kids got in from school and we'd move to a smaller house and reduce our mortgage. I just wanted us to start living again before it was too late.*

Another mum wrote:

> *I don't know how it happened but we just got used to an extra income for things like a second holiday and meals out. When I realised I was practically*

having a nervous breakdown and missing my kids growing up into the bargain, for the sake of two weeks in Majorca and a couple of curries, I sat down and cried and then laughed. I still work, but nothing like those old hours.

Somebody has said that motherhood is 'guilt-edged insecurity'. But most mums don't need more guilt. Susan is a mum of two small children aged three and five. She doesn't go to work to chase unnecessary money. She works so her family can make ends meet. She doesn't need more guilt, she needs more support – from her husband and from the government – support that will allow her to make choices that are best for her and her children; choices that will help her enjoy, instead of just enduring her motherhood. It's the right of every mother.

The Lure of the Illusions

And, finally, as we come to the close of this section, I've already mentioned that when my kids were small I made many mistakes in terms of over-commitment. I have spent years talking to fathers about three illusions that kept me in that lifestyle far longer than I should have been. I don't presume they will be relevant to your situation, but they just might be.

The first illusion was that I used to say to myself, 'I'm doing this for them – I want them to have more than I had.' It may be a noble sentiment; the problem with it is that most kids would far prefer fewer 'things' and more of us. One child psychologist put it well: 'We are so busy giving our kids what we didn't have, we don't have time to give them what we *did* have.'

The second illusion was that life would not always be so busy. I would tell myself that this pressurised period would soon pass and then I would have more time for the things that really mattered. The truth is that for most of us this is not a busy period – this is life. Until we realise this, we'll be forever putting off things that really matter to us with the promise that there will be time . . . tomorrow.

And the third illusion was that the door of childhood would be open for ever. I believed that when I said to the kids, 'later' or 'we'll do it next weekend', that there always would be a 'later'. But there comes a time when they don't really want to do things with us. They still love us, but if we think that chances to tell stories and play board games will last for ever, we may be kidding ourselves.

But let the final words on this whole issue go to a working mother. Her name is Mary Bourgoin.

A Letter from America

These days it seems that my city is one of weary women, or, more accurately, exhausted working mothers. For several months I have been amongst those who rise at dawn to shower, blow dry their hair, pack lunches, do a load of washing, iron a few shirts, and glance at the morning paper to make sure the world is not ending before 9.00 a.m.

Provided there is no last-minute scramble for missing shoes, homework, and the hamster isn't lost, my three daughters are at school by 8.40 a.m. and I am on my way to the 'real world'.

My job is interesting: working on Capitol Hill as a journalist, investigating the legal process, interviewing members of Congress – all described in my old school magazine under the heading, 'Mary Bourgoin's Glamorous Job!' The only problem is that most of the time I feel that I have one foot on a banana peel and the other on ice.

Balancing marriage, motherhood and career has become the classic women's problem of modern life. For those who can pull it all together, life is a first-class act. But judging from my own experience and from talking with other women, life is often a constant round of heartburn, ulcers, and anxiety attacks.

During the past decade more and more women have entered the labour force. Although much discussion about career opportunities for women focuses on personal growth and fulfilment, the fact is that the majority of women work because they need the money.

Yet it seems that my generation has now romanticised careers as the cure-all for identity crisis, the supermum syndrome, the housewife blues, and the empty-nest heartache. Replacing the happy housewife heroine is the successful business woman who climbs up the corporate ladder without chipping her nail polish, who breezes through the day wearing immaculately tailored clothes, and who returns home, hairdo intact, to an adoring husband, and two well-adjusted children.

The sad and obvious truth is that a great many women are now finding out what men have always known – dead-end jobs abound, most work eventually becomes boring, bosses, colleagues, and clients can be demanding, irritating and nasty, and it is just as easy to feel trapped and unhappy sitting in a posh office amid the trappings of success as it is standing in the kitchen surrounded by whining preschoolers.

The truth is that the breezy you-can-do-it-all articles leave out an important factor – energy. 'Motherhood', as somebody has said, 'saps the energy.' And so does a high-pressure career where upward job mobility is a way of life.

Marriage is also demanding, requiring inner strength and motivation to keep a relationship from going stale. Simply put, when it comes to energy, physical or emotional, we have only so much.

I am weary of magazine articles about the successful dynamic mother-wife career wonder-woman. Something is missing. The unglamorous parts are air-brushed out. The stories bear no relation to reality.

The tales I hear from women – conversations on the underground, concerns over coffee, instructions whispered over the phone to children, husbands, baby-sitters, teachers – describe the edited-out scenes; sick children sent to school or left home alone, baby-sitters who permit their charges to watch endless hours of television, sleeping babies who are awakened at 6.00 a.m. and delivered to day care centres at 7.00 a.m., the growing number of latchkey

children – eight- and nine-year-olds who are left
unsupervised on their own after school until a parent
returns home – the endless makeshift arrangements
for the dreaded school holidays, teacher in-set days,
and schools closed because of snow.

My mother was poor; she was a seamstress in a
shirt factory. She knew all too well the reality of the
world of working mothers. 'Work,' my mother often
says watching from the sidelines as I try successive
variations of my marriage-career-children juggling
act, 'is terribly overrated.'

One recent evening on my way home from work,
bone tired, worried about my equally busy husband,
a melancholy daughter and a cantankerous boss,
I came across a newspaper article about several
celebrity women.

'It's nifty', said one, 'that women are no longer
bound by traditional role models and careers.' Yes, I
agreed, and yet I had the feeling that she was naively
enthusiastic about the 'new woman' viewing the
world through the wrong end of the binoculars.
When one panellist described how she manages to
do it all my doubts turned to convictions. She said,
'My husband and I both work at home. We have a
year-old child whose care is shared equally between
the two of us and a nurse.'

I was too tired to laugh.[5]

It's almost impossible to be able to discuss these issues
without being polarised either as somebody who wants
to release women from the ties of homemaking or as
somebody who wants to tighten the knots. The truth is

that now women are increasingly able to pursue work outside the home, the responsibility of giving support to those who make that choice involves us all – partners, employers and government. But the only sensible way to do that is against a background where the task of staying at home to care for children is given dignity, and those who make that choice are given the support they need as well.

Above all we need to remember the proverb I mentioned above: 'If we do this, we can't do that.' Life may not be quite as 'modern' as we think. Although much in society has changed, life still comes with more or less the same package of responsibilities as it always did: our relationships need time and attention, as do the kids; the food needs to be bought and cooked, the rent or mortgage needs to be paid, and we need to find a little time to reproduce.

The issue of whether to work outside the home, and if so how much, and how to split responsibilities between partners, is not easy to resolve. For many there will be no choice. But whatever you decide, don't be plagued by what others think. Do what you consider right for you and your family. But don't be too tired to laugh.

Sixty Second Wisdom
(from a mother of four)

When your test kit turns blue remember:

60 you've got nine months to get used to the idea;

60 at least you'll get a seat on the bus;

60 it'll be the baby's first time too – you can learn together;

60 you can eat king-size Mars bars – how will anyone know?

60 you can get your fillings done free.

Things Mothers Say . . .

- I wish someone had told me that glowing mother love is not automatically delivered with the baby and you don't feel like the mum on the baby food advert who has time to roll around on a white bed-cover in her size eight jeans with a peaceful, gurgling baby. You feel tired, sore, frightened and completely overwhelmed by responsibility hormones. You fight with your partner more than ever. And I wish someone had said that all this is normal.

- You have to be there for them. Whatever they do, wherever they go, even if they've really hurt you – you still have to be there for them.

- You never stop being a mother. When they've grown up and left home, you have no authority over them at all and you can't do anything about it when they make mistakes. You just have to let them go; but when they leave, part of you goes with them.

You're Not the Only Mother Who . . .

- Spends three hours and the entire weekly food budget on a really special meal for them all, only to have it greeted with questions like, 'What's this green stuff?' and 'Can I have cheese on toast?' And you lock yourself in the toilet, wipe away a tear, and ask yourself why it matters so much, and why it hurts so much. But you never quite know.

- Says, 'If ever I leave home, it will surely be at a quarter past five.'

- Climbs into one of their empty beds at three in the morning because they've all climbed into yours when they got scared in the night. You've heard all the advice about settling them back into their beds so they'll know there's nothing to fear, but you've already spent half the night with your head leaning on the bedside table. That 2-foot 6-inch bed with the Beatrix Potter duvet looks just fine.

Anxious Mum

I walked painfully into the house while Mark lifted the baby seat out of the car and carried it into the sitting-room. I gazed down at my sleeping new-born son, hoping the sniffly sound in his nose wasn't anything to worry about. There were no nurses to ask now – we'd brought him home from the maternity hospital after just two days, and it was up to us to get it right.

I didn't get much sleep that night – not that Sam kept me awake. He only woke once. But I had to keep looking at him, putting a hand on his back to feel his body rise and fall, checking he was still breathing.

I lost count of the times I took Sam to the clinic or the doctor, or requested home visits in the first year of his life. It was only when I had my second baby, Beth, three years later, that I realised how much I'd worried. I even had to be reminded to take Beth to the clinic to be weighed, and as for home visits from the doctor, they were a thing of the past. I feel embarrassed now as I remember my anxiety over Sam – but I know the medical profession is used to it and didn't mind. 'Another first-time mother,' they probably said to each other.

Chapter 5
When a Mother Is Alone

Some years ago I was invited to take part in a seminar on relationships in the family. It was the coffee interval, I was the next speaker, and I was sitting on the edge of the stage waiting for my turn. Suddenly a woman approached me; she was about thirty-five years old, and had obviously been crying. She sat next to me and I asked her what was wrong.

She explained that the previous speaker had stressed the importance of a father in the life of a child. She turned to me and said, 'My children, a boy and a girl, have no father, he left years ago. Are they destined to fail? My son is causing me a lot of worry at the moment.' I felt tremendous compassion for her.

Nobody believes more strongly than I that, if possible, it's best for a child to have a mother and a father. But it's sad if, in making that basic point, we make single parents not only feel second-class but suggest they are doomed to failure. I listened for a while and then said, 'I don't know you, but you sound like a fantastic mother; your kids are fortunate; don't believe for another second that they are certain to fail.' I gave her the number of an organisation that works to help and support single parents and said, 'You *will* make it.'

A month later I got a letter:

Thank you so much for the time you spent with me. You will never know what it meant to me. You gave me hope. I took notes of some of the things you said in your talk and when I got back I made a short presentation to a parenting group in my church. I have never spoken in public before and I was so nervous, but halfway through I looked up and saw my fifteen-year-old son standing at the back listening. When it was over, he came straight up to me, put his arms around me and said, 'Mum – you were fantastic!'

These days I never begin one of our seminars without specifically welcoming those who are single parents. I believe they have the hardest job on the face of the earth. A friend of mine who is a single-parent mum overheard another mother talking about people like her: 'I've got no time for single parents. They're a problem, their children are trouble. It's their own fault anyway. They have children by different fathers and expect us to keep them.' The reality is far from that. The latest statistics show that less than ten per cent of single mothers are under the age of twenty. Sixty per cent have been married, and nine per cent of single parents are fathers. And there are many kinds of single parents. Some have experienced the death of a partner; others have known divorce or desertion. Some have gone ahead with a pregnancy knowing almost from day one there would never be a father's presence and support. Some single parents – usually mothers – have custody of their children; others may see them on weekends only. Many have known unimaginable hurt. One mother wrote to me telling me what life had been like for her and her children.

> *Over the years there were repeated affairs, use of pornography, violence, control etc. In between each crisis he was a different man. He lived a Jekyll and Hyde existence, and the children suffered because they never knew who he was. Since he left, my daughter has told me she used to brace herself as she walked downstairs every morning and was so relieved if he was 'nice' daddy. The only thing she has questioned was why I didn't ask him to go years ago. She has been so hurt. 'Why can't I have a daddy like other girls?' she said once. 'And I don't mean Dad – he's never been a Daddy to me.'*

I spoke to the mother who wrote that letter. She told me that of course she wanted her children to have a father who loved them and cared for them. But that wasn't an option for them; survival was.

Carole is another typical example of somebody who honestly believed that single parenthood would never be an issue for her. She had been married for five years and was eight months pregnant when her husband, Paul, left her for the woman he had been having an affair with for the previous two months. I have no idea what attitude Carole had towards single-parent mums before this trauma hit her, but she summed up what so many face when, just before the birth of her baby, she said, 'All the joy of having this child is gone. He won't be there when the baby is born. There will be lots of other issues too – like leaving the baby at home because I'll have to work to pay the mortgage. I'm just not sure I can do it all alone.'

And every single-parent mum or dad will have heard through the media what research has shown with regard to their children's behaviour and prospects; without doubt it is better for a child to have a mother and a father. But what so often doesn't come across is the tenacity, sheer dedication and hope that most single parents have. The lone parent often has to do battle on half a dozen fronts at once. Although she knows she can't do it, she is trying to be both a mother and a father to this child.

Money is often tight but the real bottom line is that you face issues big and small – alone. It doesn't matter whether it's a blocked sink, a teenager experimenting with drugs, a car with a flat battery or a lump in the breast. You have somehow to deal with it – yourself. But added to that, and perhaps worst of all, is that you don't know whether the difficulties you are experiencing are the normal ones that every mother is going through, or whether it really is because your child doesn't have a father around at home. At times you are fit to burst; you spend half your life worrying about what's happened and the other half worrying about what might happen.

A couple of years ago Dianne was away and I was holding the fort. Lloyd was usually pretty good about getting in on time, but on this occasion he was due to be in by midnight and there was no sign of him. It's a scenario that every parent of teenagers understands completely. At about 12.05 I started to panic. At 12.15 I made myself a cup of tea and told myself not to be stupid.

At 12.25 I thought, 'This is common – think what you were like when you were young.' That really panicked me. At 12.45 I started rifling drawers for Lloyd's friends' telephone numbers. At 12.50 I descended into a spiral of panic from which there was no escape. I was sure that the sirens I could hear in the distance were on top of ambulances conveying my son to hospital, or that any moment I would see a blue light flash in the street outside.

When he eventually came in, I didn't know whether to hug him or ground him until his late forties. And then I realised that this is what single parents go through every day of the week. It's not that there aren't friends and family who care, it's just that in the everyday business of parenting, whatever they face – they face alone.

One single-parent mum summarised the difficulties.

Twenty-four-hour parenting

There's no one else when you've just had enough. Even ordinary things can seem like mountains to climb. I'm scared of getting flu because somebody has to care for my kids. The other day I had to go into hospital for a minor operation but first I had to get somebody to have my two children for a couple of days. You'd think it would be easy but sometimes it seems impossible.

Pain

At the same time as trying to be Supermum you are trying to cope with the terrible pain of being left alone – a whole bundle of emotions – anger, grief, rejection

— and sometimes sheer bewilderment. The worst part is when the kids say, 'If daddy had loved us he wouldn't have left.'

Money

It's often hand-to-mouth. I work outside the home part-time but even so we don't have much. I don't care so much about myself but I want them to have what other kids have.

There's just nobody to talk to . . .

Nobody to say, 'Don't be daft' or 'Let the baby cry for a while' or 'You're doing a great job'. I so often have the sense that I really am on my own.

Lynda Hunter, who is a single-parent mum with three children, wrote to me and shared some of the lessons she had learnt.

The other day, I forgot that my daughter had to stay behind for a drama rehearsal and I spent the best part of an hour waiting for her outside her school. As I sat in the car on that warm August afternoon, my mind went back fourteen years when, while paying bills, I found an unusually large hotel receipt from a business trip my husband had taken. I called the hotel for an explanation. Their reply changed my life for ever: my husband was having an affair. When I confronted him, he simply walked away from our marriage, notwithstanding the fact that our girls were only three and one year old, and I was pregnant with our son.

The next few months became a blur as the baby came and I was served with divorce papers. For some reason I can't understand, I felt ashamed, and, for reasons I can understand – completely broken. The only thing I wanted to do was to hide in the house and let the world pass me by. And then one day I saw my son roll over in his cot for the first time. It struck me that his young life was already afflicted with heartache but he didn't know that and he was just getting on with making progress. How could I do any less?

As I sat in the car, fourteen years on, I asked myself, 'What helped me get on with the business of living? What lessons have I learnt as a single mother?'

The first is the most profound and was the most difficult to learn: I could not be a father to my children; I could only be the best mother I could possibly be. We all want the best for our children, and so many of us single parents feel we must compensate for the loss of a father. But we can only do so much. You just can't be mum and dad. One way I have got over that is to welcome the involvement of men that I trust in my children's lives. Of course these are normally professionals – it could be a teacher, a youth leader, or sports coach. The alternative is to reinforce the belief that because one man has let us down, there are no good ones out there. I don't believe it and more important I don't want them to believe it. I welcome any help that I can trust, in the task of bringing up these kids.

I also discovered that sometimes I didn't get help because I didn't ask for it. I am very independent and to be honest I felt enough of a failure already, but I discovered that if I made my needs known other people would help: they would pick up the kids from school occasionally; dads who lived nearby would make sure to include my son when they took their kids to football matches; friends would occasionally baby-sit so I could get a break. But if I didn't ask, people assumed I was doing all right.

Perhaps the biggest thing is that I shook off the guilt. I did all I could to keep my marriage from falling apart. Sure I'd made mistakes, but I couldn't bear total responsibility – that would crush me. I had somehow, for my kids' sake, to try to put the past behind me and live each day as it came. Part of that, for me, was forgiveness. I know it sounds strange, but one day I sat in the kitchen and wrote down every hurtful thing my husband had ever done to me. I held the list in my hands and cried, and then I asked God to help me forgive. When I was done, I burnt the paper. Of course I still remember those hurts, but somehow I feel free of my ex-husband's power over me. I have tried to forgive him and in the process somehow got free myself. I never criticise him to the kids – he is still their father – turning them against him won't help me or them.

Then I concentrated on the positives. My kids have a mother who loves them and who wants to spend time with them. I know from watching the busy lives of some two-parent families that my kids get more of my time than many of their friends do from their parents. Single parenthood focuses you. I'm not working to get the latest car. I'm working as little as I can to make ends meet and when I'm not working I'm with those kids.

I accepted the fact that I am not the perfect mother and even more – that many of the issues I went through with my children, whether it was a toddler having tantrums, a child who hated school, or a teenager who's giving everybody a hard time – are normal. Almost every mother – single parent or not – faces these things. In other words I stopped beating myself up for no good reason.

And finally I learnt that, although money was almost always tight, most children prefer a parent's time to expensive toys. I couldn't give my kids the latest computers, bikes or televisions in their bed-room, and so I had to find ways to somehow make up for that. We discovered that doing simple things together – learning to cook, building a den in the garden, sometimes even bargain-hunting in second-hand shops, was a lot more fun than sitting in front of a computer. Above all, my children and I learned to laugh together. I have wonderful kids – that doesn't stop them being kids – driving me crazy with worry at times – but our trouble has brought us close. We are there for each other.

As I was still trundling back through the years, my seventeen-year-old daughter tapped on the car window and jerked me back to reality. She said, 'You were miles away, Mum.'

I gazed at her and thought, 'It has turned out

better than I dared hope. But you will never know, at times, how very hard it's been.'

'Oh,' I said, 'I was just reminiscing.'

'Well, don't,' she replied. 'What's for dinner?'

Sixty Second Wisdom

Understand 'teenspeak' . . .

60 *You say:* 'You look nice dear.'
She thinks: 'I must look naff! I'll change.'

60 *You say:* 'He's a nice boy.'
She thinks: 'How can I dump him kindly?'

60 *You say:* 'Have you got enough money?'
She thinks: 'Has Ivana Trump?'

60 *You say:* 'Get home at a sensible time.'
She thinks: 'Six a.m.'s sensible for milkmen.'

Why Did I Worry?

Why did I worry that he should be first to:

    sleep through the night
    point to his nose
    say 'Hello Dad'
    eat with a fork
    sleep in a bed
    sign his name
    learn the piano

When at seventeen he:

    sleeps through the day
    pierces his nose
    grunts at his Dad
    eats with his fingers
    sleeps on the floor
    calls himself Zog
    plays the bongo?

Why was I anxious that he wouldn't:

tell the time
learn to swim
get to make friends
cross the road safely
learn the value of money
be attractive to girls
want to know me

When at seventeen he:

is always in at 2 a.m.
spends every summer Saturday at the beach
has an address book as thick as
a telephone directory
is off to India this summer
earns more than I do at his part-time job
appears to have a harem
still (occasionally) gives me a hug?

Mothers' Race

Watching the line-up for the mothers' race on sports day is a good way of reminding yourself of the diversity of motherhood style. There are usually one or two 'Competitive Carlas'. They've been training for weeks under cover of darkness, and they intend to WIN. Just the same way that they expect their kids to ... every time.

Next to them you'll see 'Slap-Dash Sophie'. She'll run in her shoes with her skirt hitched up (her child's the one with his hands over his face). She'll run happily along and probably arrive last without making too much effort and doesn't really care what anyone thinks.

Then there's 'Tell-Them-How-To-Do-It Tina'. She misses the starting-gun because she's busy telling the next two in the line how to run the race. When she gets to the end in tenth place, it's someone else's fault and she'll talk about the unfairness of the race all the way home.

'Keeping-Up-Appearances Kerry' runs because she wants to be seen to do the right thing. She's desperate to get on to the PTA committee but her anxious expression, shared by all three of her children, tends to make other mums wary of her. She will genuinely lose sleep if she is placed further down the rank than third.

'All-Right-Then Ann' is the one who was persuaded to join in by her two boys against her better judgment. She hardly ever runs – let alone in a straight line – but she doesn't want to let them down. She throws her shoes into the long-jump pit just before the race and will probably lose them, but who cares, this is for the expression on those two faces! She runs as fast as she knows how and is genuinely surprised to find herself come in second. Her triumph earns much laughter at the supper table.

Perhaps she's the only one who takes time to find comparisons between the race today and the mothering she does. It's all over too quickly, she thinks. There are no real winners or losers and training doesn't make much difference. You just have to get on and do it the best way you can, in your own style, and watch the expressions on those little faces. And, above all, hope with all your heart that just as 'Competitive Carla' is about to break the tape, she trips and goes headlong into the orange squash stall.

Shopping

I am in my late forties and took my daughter aged fourteen to get myself a new outfit for a wedding. You know what it's like; I had trudged around store after store but finally I found something I thought was really nice. As I slipped into it in the changing room, I felt really good. I emerged to get my daughter's verdict. She looked up from her magazine and said, 'No – it's too young for your face.'

You're not the only mother who . . .

. . . when your second baby arrives, abandons all those great ideals you had with the first:

- You didn't let the first one suck his fingers, let alone the cat's tail.

- You gave the first one organic baby rice – this one survives on chocolate spread on toast.

- You changed the first if he dribbled down his bib – this poor kid looks like an extra on *Oliver Twist*.

Chapter 6

When a Mother Is Sick

– *Wendy Bray*

Just before Wendy began helping me with this book, she discovered she had cancer. Most mothers will not experience what she is going through but, nevertheless, difficult times hit us all. This is the shortest chapter in the book, but may well contain the deepest lessons.

When each of my two children were born I looked down at their pink wrinkled faces in the knowledge that I was their Mum; that I would always love them, care for them and protect them, to the best of my ability. It seemed a certainty, a right, a privilege. When, earlier this year, I was diagnosed with an advanced aggressive cancer, everything changed. The certainty of my care was shaken. The right to be there for them was suddenly removed and the privilege of mothering them grew to incredible proportions. Now I have to consider that although there is a strong possibility that I *will* carry on mothering them, that I *will* be there for them in six months, two years, ten years, there is an equally strong possibility that I *will not*. That I will die as my son starts secondary school and my daughter moves further into her teenage years. That I won't be around just at the time when, in many ways, they will need me most, leaving my husband, family and friends to guide them through those difficult years without me.

Suddenly even the mistakes I've made as a mum seem precious as I realise that the 'rights' and 'certainties' of motherhood were probably never there anyway – just the privileges and responsibilities.

It is as if 'normal motherhood', if there is such a thing, is Plan A, but I have to find a Plan B. The insurance back up. The contingency plan. Plan B is impossible to find because there is no insurance policy for a mother's love. All I can do is build in them the resources, the skills, the faith, the love and simple wisdom they will need to live. With or without me. Love them and laugh with them now in the hope that I can go on loving and laughing with them.

For now at least, I am not afraid of the cancer. I am not afraid of death. I know that all of us as a family are in the palm of God's hand. He knows what I *am* afraid of. It's when, in my imagination, I can hear the children calling for me in the distance just as they have many times over the past thirteen years. Their calling 'Mum' has become like a familiar tune with many variations. Calling for attention; calling for help; calling to ask if tea is ready or to share a joke. But in this dream they keep on calling. Their cries become more and more desperate, wondering why I'm not responding. But I can't get there. Somebody else has to go and comfort them and tell them that Mum can't come. Until they understand that Mum never *will* come. Then there is the empty, overwhelming feeling that breaks my heart that I have let them down.

How would I have responded as I held those two newborns if somebody had told me about that dream? Would I have handed them back? Said I'd changed my mind? Demanded a rewrite of the story? No. Because we are called to mother whatever the circumstances. We only have to watch the news to understand how many are mothering 'against the odds' at the risk of great pain.

I don't think the experience of the last months has made me value the children more or take them less for granted as might be expected. Perhaps I was already aware of the brevity of their childhood. But it *has* made me realise that there is a hidden quality of love enveloped in difficult circumstances of which only a few will have a privileged glimpse. A kind of velvet lining to a broken vessel which infuses the day-to-day with something special.

Mothering is all about facing the pain and mothering *anyway*. Loving *anyway*, laughing *anyway*. And thankfully, there is still more than enough to laugh at. I still look down at their pink wrinkled faces – when they're giggling. In all the sadness and seriousness of the issues we're facing, the giggling never stops. Who would want it to!

Chapter 7
When a Mother Feels Guilty

Motherhood is a risky business because mothers get blamed for the ills of the world. Even when, by any standards, these women have given love and commitment until it is coming out of their ears, somebody is always near at hand to point out the deficiency in potty-training, discipline or education that has ruined their kids' lives. These mothers are either too laid-back or over possessive; they have robbed their kids of their time by going out to work, or bored them to death by staying at home; they left teaching them to read too late, or killed their love of books by pushing them too young; and if they hadn't skipped pages when they used to read those bedtime stories this child would have passed English GCSE.

It's hard to take that kind of pressure without it getting to you. As I talk to mothers, I find that time and time again the same word keeps coming up – 'guilt'. All sorts of mums – young ones, old ones, stay-at-home, out-to-work, and single mums – say the same thing. Typical comments are:

- I've lost confidence in my ability to parent.
- It's too late to go back and put it right.
- I'm overwhelmed by the responsibility of it all.

One mother summed it all up:

> *It's a disease prevalent among mothers. You'll recognise the symptoms when you hear phrases such as: 'I'm sorry but . . .' or 'I know I ought to but . . .' If you ask a mother if she goes out to work, she might reply: 'No, I'm only a housewife and mother,' or perhaps, 'Yes, I do – but it's only part-time, and she really loves going to the child-minder, and I'm always back for bedtime, and we have quality time together when I'm not at work . . .'*
>
> *The disease is called guilt. We sufferers feel the need to justify ourselves to others, to apologise for our actions, and to constantly compare our own shortcomings to those of other people. It starts when you're a mum-to-be. You feel you shouldn't have had that glass of wine/run for the bus/painted the bedroom ceiling on your own – because it might be bad for the baby. But the guilt reaches its ante-natal height in the delivery room. You should be able to manage without gas and air/pethidine/ epidural – on no account should you have a Caesarean.*
>
> *After the birth it gets worse. Your baby is the only one in the hospital who cries through the night and keeps everyone else awake. You know you ought to breast-feed like everyone else but you simply can't.*

You must have your washing-up done and be out of your dressing gown before the health visitor arrives at 10.00 a.m.

And so it goes on. The guilt grows with the child, reaching peaks when everybody else's child is potty-trained first and seems to reach all the other milestones earlier too. You should have put her name down earlier for that really good school – now her whole future career is spoilt because you were too late. You should have been there for sports day – even though it was your grandmother's funeral that afternoon. You should have noticed that this wasn't just teenage angst and wanting time off school – it was actually glandular fever.

You're guilty because you leave your child and go out to work while the woman next door is an at-home mum. What you don't realise is that the woman next door is feeling guilty because she isn't contributing to the family income and because she is 'only' a housewife, and she's feeling inadequate because she watches how well you cope with career and family! Why can't we decide what's right for us as a family, and go ahead and do it – whether it's breast-feeding, going back to work, moving house, having another child – without worrying so much? Answer: because we're mothers, and motherhood goes with guilt like a horse with a carriage.

I am tempted to say, for the sake of equality, that guilt also affects many fathers, but in my experience this is often much later – usually when they look back after their children are grown and perhaps wish they had been more involved. For many women, however, mother-guilt becomes a way of life. I don't think we should be surprised by this; modern mothers face special pressures that can easily lead to a sense of failure.

Pressure Number One: Expectations

My father died aged eighty-five, and my mother is now ninety. Without doubt they were good parents, but it may just be that the parenthood examination was a little easier then. I can't remember my father reading me bedtime stories, or spending vast amounts of time with me, or speaking to me about my future, my love-life, or teaching me woodwork. Was he a good disciplinarian? The answer is hard to give, because for some reason that is not now immediately apparent, we obeyed him without question. My father not only rarely smacked us, he rarely shouted. In fact if he lifted his eyebrow over the newspaper you knew you were in a lot of trouble. Did we have a close relationship with him? Probably not. Did he love us? Certainly, although he rarely told us so.

So how come I look back and say, 'He was a good father'? The answer is, 'Because the expectations were different then.' He saw his role as that of the breadwinner and the disciplinarian. He worked for fifty years and in all that time had only eleven days off due to sickness. There was always food on the table and clothes on our back.

Did my father ever feel guilty as a parent? Of course I don't really know, but I would be staggered to discover that he even thought about it. My mother worked hard both inside and outside the home, and showered us with affection. Did she ever feel guilty? Again, I doubt it – perhaps only that we didn't have as much in terms of material possessions as other kids.

How different for today's parents. We live in a world where we are used to seeing pop stars, football players, and mass-murderers lay the blame for any difficulties they encounter at the feet of their parents. We begin to imagine our children on some morning television chat show blowing the gaff on us. It's not difficult to be worried. We look at other families and we are sure their children are more polite, have tidier bedrooms, and do their homework more diligently than ours. And then fear takes over. Our mind begins to run away with us and we think, 'Today it's just a late homework assignment, but he'll probably fail all his exams, he doesn't eat properly, his bedroom is a mess, he is going to ruin his life.'

If we don't do something to halt these runaway fears they can immobilise us. This is so because we begin to lose confidence in our parenting. We are constantly saying to ourselves things like, 'I dealt with that badly' or 'I've blown it again' or 'If I hadn't lent her the money to go out she'd never have met that dreadful boy'. Even worse, we begin to see those events as irretrievable – the damage is done – for ever. The truth is, we do blow it as parents and we do deal with things badly, but we're learning on the job as well.

The real killer is when we come to believe that parents who get it right (whatever that is) would have dealt with a situation in a certain way. Imagine that your fifteen-year-old daughter was meant to be home at eleven-thirty and she rolls in at one o'clock. You say to her, 'You're grounded for a month.' She yells, she spits, and says she hates you. And the following day, while shopping, you meet a mother who seems to have perfect children who says, 'Oh no, I would never do that. This is what you should have said to her: "You are almost an adult and I am being unreasonable. Could we agree to twelve o'clock next time?" ' As you leave the post-office queue you notice you are talking to yourself, 'She's right – I blew it – I should have reasoned with her.'

And at that very moment you meet Cathy whom everybody knows has a PhD in motherhood. She shakes her head when she hears the advice suggested by the post office woman and whispers in your ear, 'The key is in the pocket money. Tell your daughter that next time you'll deduct fifty pence for every ten minutes that she's late.' You thank her profusely and rush off dying to try it, until you suddenly have a vision of your daughter coming in at two-thirty in the morning, handing you ten pounds and saying, 'That should cover it, Mum.'

Your head is whirling – what should you do? The answer is that you should probably go with your original instincts – you know your daughter better than anybody else. The reality is that most 'solutions' have to be changed, adapted or renegotiated as the years go by. If one strategy doesn't work, try something else. We have somehow to stop the guilt, caused by unrealistic expectations, that can rob us of the confidence to parent our children.

Pressure Number Two: Isolation

Dianne has got an inspirational poster on our kitchen wall. Having said that, it's not your normal run-of-the-mill affair; you know the sort of thing, 'Today is the first day of the rest of your life.' She used to have that hanging there and then one teatime, when she was standing ankle-deep in water because the washing machine had died, with five fish fingers nicely on fire in the frying pan, and Lloyd telling her he'd lost the hamster, she apparently thought, 'No – if the rest is like the first day, you can keep it.' Lots of her inspirational posters have been binned around teatime, but one has remained.

I'm sure the artist didn't intend it to lift mothers' spirits, or help them to face another day, but Dianne tells me this is what it does for her every time she looks at it. It's set somewhere in the early fifties; there's a row of small terraced houses, and two women are leaning on a garden wall. They both have scarves around their heads and look as if they've just got back from an afternoon shift at work. But now they are taking time to just talk. A small scruffy boy with a huge smile is looking up at one of the women, but they ignore him; this is *their* time.

I asked Dianne what it is that she finds so uplifting about the picture. She said that as she looks at it she imagines herself in that garden and eavesdropping on the conversation . . .

One woman is complaining because her old man seems to be dying of flu but the second he gets into bed suddenly recovers wonderfully and wants sex. The other throws her head back and laughs before she shares that her teenage son has stopped using language; he grunts his way around the house, and won't be seen dead with her outside of it. Just then in my mind's eye I see that the brand-new mum from the house along the terrace ventures into her garden and one of the older women shouts across three garden walls, 'How's the little one, love?' The younger woman looks up red-eyed, and says, 'He just won't sleep – he cries all night. I haven't slept since half-past two.' The old hands laugh, 'Listen, my love – make sure he's fed, warm and dry – but don't pick him up every time he cries – if you do, you'll be doing it when he's thirty!' 'Like Mrs Tompkin's boy!' shrieks the other. (Rumour has it Arthur Tompkin is still breast-feeding at thirteen.) The young mum smiles, then laughs, and makes her way back to do battle with a four-week-old, but I sense her head is held a little higher.

I think Dianne is right – the conversation, the laughter was liberating. I'm not naive enough to believe those were the 'golden days' but they did have one great advantage then: families normally lived closer than they do today. You tended to bring up your children surrounded by other mothers – your own mother, aunties, grandmothers and friends. Knowledge and experience were passed on, and also something far more important: the understanding that whatever you were going through with your kids had been gone through before. You were neither unique in your success nor, more important, alone in your failure.

From what they tell me, most mothers don't want clever answers, and they certainly don't want clever answers from those who pretend they've got it all sorted. What they want most of all is for another mother to whisper to them, 'This isn't just you – we've all been there, done it and worn the tee-shirt.' One mum said:

> *I discovered I could handle almost all motherhood could throw at me so long as somebody could reassure me when I felt I'd screwed it up completely and ruined my kids' lives for ever, that probably there had been other children who gave up violin after the first lesson, got caught smoking behind the toilets in school, and altered their school report on the way home.*

The good thing about this particular pressure is that we can do something about it. But to achieve this we have to realise that two of the most helpful words we can hear when we are doubting our ability as parents are 'me too'. We somehow have to learn to share not just our successes but our failures with others. The strange thing is that when we do, we find we don't depress those parents – we make their day!

Pressure Number Three: The Experts

I write books on family life and run seminars on parenting and so I acknowledge that I'm part of the problem, but we have a proliferation of gurus on the family. These men and women often have a lot to teach us, and we would do well to consider what they say. Without doubt parenting is harder today than in previous generations, and we need all the help we can get. But the problem comes when we take what they say too seriously. By this I mean attaching to their advice the status of infallibility. The difficulty with this is there will always be somebody talking about some aspect of parenting, and suggesting ideas that either it's too late for us to try, or we know in our heart just won't work in our situation. One mother put it like this: 'Every time I hear a parenting expert giving a "foolproof" way to deal with kids, I try it, only to discover that mine are the exception to the rule.'

Take a common example. Most experts agree that it's unwise to pick up your newborn baby every time she cries and, even worse, to allow that to get to the stage where she sleeps in your bed when she's a toddler. There are many good reasons why that's not a good idea, not least in the area of your ongoing sanity. But the truth is that there are millions of perfectly well-adjusted kids whose mothers did exactly that. These mums tried hanging around outside the bedroom door while their babies yelled their heads off, but they just couldn't do it. So what? Are those mums condemned to believe that they have ruined for ever their child's chance of developing independence? Well, if you are one of them, hang on, because there's sure to be a guru out there who will soon be saying, 'The best way to build a sense of security in your child is to pick her up every time she cries . . .'

I am not saying we don't need help as parents – I spend a fair part of my life organising parenting courses – it's just that when we've read the books, listened to the health visitor, been to the seminars and watched the parenting videos, we have to decide what works for *us*. And above all we need to remember that children are people, not machines. We sometimes wish it were different but every mother has to be ready to put past failures behind her, try new things and sometimes pray and hope for the best, because every child is different and we are learning all the time. The other day Dianne was speaking at a seminar and I heard her say this:

> When I was six months pregnant with Katie I remember saying, 'I'm not sure I'm ready to have this baby.' I'm confident that many women have felt like that, but you know the really strange thing is that I now have more than twenty years of parenting behind me, I've got two kids through teething, toddlerhood, and the terrible teens, Rob and I have spoken to tens of thousands of people on parenting issues, and yet, if I was pregnant tomorrow, I can still imagine saying, 'Rob, I don't think I'm ready to have this baby.'
>
> Perhaps that is not so strange for I'm not at all sure that we can 'learn' motherhood, we can only experience it, only feel it. I'm not saying that learning parenting skills or reading books on bringing up children are not helpful; Rob and I have benefited enormously by doing exactly that. It's just that sometimes we can be overwhelmed by the experts and all the advice. I believe that many mums spend their lives feeling utter failures. Some friends of ours went to visit relatives who lived hundreds of miles from us. The couple they were visiting were going through some minor hassles with their kids and when our friends happened to say they knew us, these people commented, 'Oh – the ones who write books on parenting? I suppose their kids are perfect.' I said, 'We should invite them to come and stay for a couple of days: they won't stop laughing for a month.'

Pressure Number Four:
It Would Be a Great Job
If It Wasn't for the Children

So many of the mothers who write to us say they feel failures and wish they could rewind the tape and have another run at parenthood. It seems to me that the great problem with bringing up children is that it's so unfair. The first child is normally quite a test, but you read a couple of books, talk to friends and eventually you feel you're beginning to get the hang of it. And that's what lures you into having the second – you think you're an expert now. The problem is that heaven in its humour looks up the kind of child it sent you last time and now delivers one that is the opposite in every characteristic. The first one used to look scared when you raised your voice; this one laughs. Number one used to love crayoning in books; number two loves crayoning on friends' wallpaper. The first one slept like a baby; this one wants to go clubbing before he's three.

And if we're not careful we think, 'I must have lost it as a parent – what's happened to me?' The truth is that probably nothing has happened, we are just going through some of the traumas that, if they were honest, most parents, including the 'experts', would admit to. Of course you may not think you are a failure; in fact you may believe you are motherhood's own success story. Even now as you sit reading this book, coffee in hand, your new baby is gurgling happily as if to say, 'Don't you worry about that next feed, and this nappy is just fine.' Your toddler has just inserted the final piece in a jigsaw that Toys R Us marked 'for children aged 10–

13', and your teenager is whistling as he finishes the dishes. Forgive me if I am about to shatter any dearly held illusions, and I am sure you are a wonderful mother, but my honest belief after observing thousands of families is that you just got lucky. My advice is, don't be tempted to have a fourth.

A Tale of Two Children

There's a gap of three years between our two children. Katie was our first and she was a typical compliant child. The first thing Katie did when she came into the world was to apologise to the midwife for being a little late. Katie was just glad to be on board. She lay on her back and gurgled as you changed her nappy, she loved to play shops, sums were a delight, she was kind to animals. And for the vast proportion of that period Dianne and I thought we were the perfect parents. We tutted to each other as we watched other toddlers having tantrums in the aisles of supermarkets. Sometimes, with hardly concealed glee, we pointed out to other parents where they might be going wrong with their offspring.

And then Lloyd came into our lives. Lloyd did not apologise to the midwife for being late. In fact Lloyd did not apologise for anything. He did not say sorry when he was three for removing the bottom can of beans from a display in Sainsbury's that I am sure took the Heinz rep a week to construct. He did not say sorry when he was five for urinating in a milk bottle in Mrs Cleverly's kitchen, or for not telling us he had done it until we had finished our coffee. Well, actually, Lloyd did say 'sorry' but it was one of those say-it-until-you-mean-it 'sorrys'.

The truth is that each of these children is unique – and they can change. Try not to break your heart over that child who is testing you daily and don't take the compliant one for granted either; there may be a little rebellion to come there too. Somebody put it well: 'Don't read your child's school reports as though they are a prophecy of their future lives.' In other words, don't read the score at half-time.

You Ain't Seen Nothing Yet

Talking of rebellion gets us into a stage of a child's life that is just perfect for making a mother feel guilty – the teenage years. If you have toddlers, I don't for one moment minimise the task you have on your hands. It was Bill Cosby who said he could conquer the world if he could mobilise about two hundred aggressive two-year-olds. And I too have stood rooted to the spot and red-faced in the aisle of a supermarket, as my toddler has created mayhem because he couldn't have that bag of sweets. The only thing I would say is that if you think this is tough, you ain't seen nothing yet. And the reason for this is that no matter how difficult your toddler is, when they are small you still have a measure of control – you can bundle him up and get him home. But the day may come when a fifteen-year-old will look you in the eye and say, 'No'. That can be scary.

And the problem is that we are used, as parents, to protecting our children – to making life right for them. But as they get older we find we cannot do that in quite the same way; we simply do not have the same measure of control. They may choose friends that we think will be a bad influence on them, they may leave homework undone, or start smoking; they may decide when they are eighteen they want to be a rock and roll singer whereas we always dreamt of their becoming a doctor. And we think, 'How has this happened? Where did I go wrong?'

It is rare to meet a parent of teenagers who does not feel in some way a failure. No matter how much we read on the topic, no matter how many television programmes we watch on parenting issues, we still believe what we are going through with our teenager is unique. A mother came up to me after one of our recent seminars. She looked troubled and obviously needed to talk. She explained that she was very concerned about her son. It seemed he'd undergone a character change. He had always been outgoing, affectionate and poured his heart out as soon as he got home from school every day. She had felt very close to him. And then he hit thirteen.

She said it was as if somebody 'had flicked a switch'. Her son seemed to change overnight. He became distant and withdrawn. Whereas before he would love to join in with whatever the family was doing, now he refused – and none too politely. He seemed to resent his parents. He shrank back when they touched him, and said he hated his mother's cooking. He spent long hours in his room, and grunted when she tried to get through to him. The only time he looked alive was when he was talking to his friends on the phone, but he soon got back to his sullen mode when he put the receiver down.

The woman sitting before me was genuinely grieving. She felt she must have done something terribly wrong when her son was young which had led to this change of character. I told her a story that I have related to thousands of mothers. Some years ago I was interviewing a very eminent child psychologist and said to him, 'Many parents of teenagers feel failures. Do you have anything to say to people like this?' The good doctor didn't hesitate. He said, 'I believe when a child reaches thirteen, hormonal changes occur in his or her body which cause them to blast into outer space. And then all communication with the satellite dies. They will only grunt at you. My advice to the parents of teenagers is just get them through those teenage years. Don't try to do much more than that. Fight as few battles as you possibly can. And then when they are about twenty, you'll begin getting signals from out there – they are still alive. And most of them land.'

And suddenly the mother in front of me started to smile; I sensed it was not with humour, but with sheer relief. It had dawned on her that what she was going through was *not just her.* She didn't mind a battle; she just wanted to be sure that she wasn't the only mother in the war.

Of course sometimes it's more serious than that. Sometimes our children break our hearts. My mind goes now to a mother who sits with her daughter in a police cell. She is saying to her, 'Rachel, I don't understand for a moment what you have done but I will always love you.' That mum loved that girl so much it hurt.

The other night I was watching *Larry King Live* when Billy Graham came on. He told of the years of heartache he and his wife Ruth endured because of the behaviour of one of his children. His son eventually came through that rocky time and Ruth has written a book about it called *Prodigals and Those Who Love Them*. But again it is the guilt that is crushing. We feel responsible even when our children are obviously old enough to make their own decisions. We ask, 'Where did I go wrong?' The answer is often, 'Nowhere'. That's not to say that we have been perfect parents, or that we wouldn't like to have done some things differently. No, it's deeper than that. It's an acknowledgment that the day comes when we can't control them. Our children make choices.

Guilt is an occupational hazard of parenthood, but maybe we can gradually loosen its hold on us. So let the last word go to a mum of two who sent me this wonderful offering:

> *Mother guilt is attached to the umbilical cord, but it stays with you for life.*
> *You feel guilty about what you do and guilty about what you don't do.*
> *Guilty when you leave them and guilty when you pick them up.*
> *Guilty about what they eat, what they don't eat and even what they might eat.*
> *The guilt gets you at night, on the train, standing in the school playground and especially when you've left them when you have a break.*
> *Then it usually gets attached to your purse and leads you to a toy shop.*
> *What mothers need is a jury of twelve good mothers and true to stand up and say 'not guilty m'lud'.*

I like that piece because it tells us we can't be the perfect parents. The most any of us can do is to give the task of parenthood our very best effort. Remember the 'Sixty Second Wisdom' from an older mother: 'Don't take all the credit; don't take all the blame.' There is a story of a man of eighty-two who was sentenced to seventeen years' imprisonment. As the judge read the punishment the defendant said, 'My Lord, I'll be almost a hundred by the time I finish; I'll never make it.' The judge hesitated, looked over the top of his half-rimmed spectacles, and said, 'Do what you can.'

It's not a bad principle for motherhood.

Sixty Second Wisdom

🔟 Don't try to control them – if you fail, you'll never see them again; if you succeed, you'll never get rid of them.

🔟 Don't ever give up – sometimes prodigals come home.

🔟 Tell your kids every day, 'I love you.'

🔟 If you want to get a child who's almost asleep fully awake, try skipping two pages of a bedtime story.

Things Mothers Say . . .

- He lives away from home now, but if you know where they are, and they keep in touch, your mind can be at rest. All he needs to do is give a quick ring and say, 'Hi Mum, I'm OK'. Most times he says, 'I've got no news', and I'll say, 'That's fine, I'm just pleased you've phoned.'

- As soon as Ben was passed to me in the delivery ward I knew he had Down's syndrome. Nobody needed to tell me. I loved him straight away and my fierce desire to protect him was there immediately. The thoughts came tumbling, 'Would I be an object of sympathy?' I didn't want people to feel sorry for me because he wasn't what they call 'normal'; that would be a rejection of my son.

- When Lynne got married and bought her first flat she brought a real smile to my face. 'Mum,' she said on the phone one day, 'we've had the gas bill, the electricity bill and the car tax all at once. You've no *idea* what it's like when they all come in together.'

Like Mother, Like Daughter

I'm forty next birthday but Mum still asks:

- 'Will you be long?'

- 'Are you warm enough?'

- 'Can't you eat something that's good for you?'

- 'Where are your slippers?'

- 'Isn't it your bedtime?'

And I say 'Yes, Mum', 'No, Mum', or, 'I'm fine, Mum'.

. . . So why does it unnerve me when I've heard myself say all these things to my teenage daughter in the last twelve hours and she's replied in exactly the same way?

Wendy

The Amnesia of Motherhood

- Helps us forget the pain of childbirth (almost), but remembers their eyes seemingly fixed on our face a few moments afterwards.

- Helps us forget the fights over food and faddy eating, but remembers cheeks and noses covered in chocolate ice cream.

- Helps us forget the clinging and crying at the nursery door or the frustration of trying to find the right school, but sits down with the memories when we find that pile of crumpled faded paintings ten years later.

- Helps us forget the arguments, the hurtful words and slammed doors, but remembers bursting with pride when they left for college or their first job and how we tried not to cry when we cleaned their empty bedroom.

Then suddenly we need to remember all those things we forgot and try to imagine what it's like for her. A new mother in a new way in a new age. Remembering that the feeling, the secret knowledge, the unique experience of mothering will never be forgotten.

She would feel her throat swell at the memory of banana sandwiches, and in the winter the smell of warm buttered toast almost made her cry. Sometimes she wondered whether it was her own childhood she mourned or the childhood of her children.

Alice Thomas Ellis, *The Other Side of the Fire*[6]

Chapter 8
When a Mother Lets Go

One of the most inspired titles I have ever come across in a book on raising children is called *Parenting Isn't for Cowards.* But it seems to me there is something more difficult than parenting: it is *not* parenting. It is the process of letting go.

We dream of the day when our children are grown and then suddenly they *are.* A mother wrote to best-selling author Erma Bombeck. She said:

> *I know you've written about the empty-nest syndrome, that lonely period after the children are grown and gone. Right now I'm up to my eyeballs in laundry and muddy boots. The baby is teething; the boys are fighting. My husband just called and said to eat without him, and my diet has crashed. Tell me about it again, will you?*

This was Erma Bombeck's reply:

> *Okay. One of these days you'll straighten up the boys' bedroom neat and tidy: bumper stickers discarded, bedspread tucked and smooth, hangers in the closet. Animals caged. And you'll say out loud,*

'Now I want it to stay that way.' And it will.

You'll say, 'I want complete privacy on the phone. No dancing around. No demolition crews. Silence! Do you hear?' And you'll have it.

No more plastic tablecloths stained with spaghetti, no more gates to stumble over at the bottom of the stairs, no more anxious nights under a vaporizer tent. No more rubber bands for pony tails or wet knotted shoestrings.

Imagine. A lipstick with a point on it. No baby-sitter for New Year's Eve. Washing only once a week. Having your teeth cleaned without a baby on your lap. No parent–teacher meetings. No blaring radios. No one washing her hair at 11.00 o'clock at night.

Think about it. No more sloppy oatmeal kisses. No more tooth fairy. No giggles in the dark. No knees to heal. No responsibility.

One of these days, you'll shout, 'Why don't you kids grow up and act your age?' And they will.[7]

I know men are not supposed to cry but if it's any comfort, a tear has just bounced off the wordprocessor. But we'd better not get too emotional about it all, simply remember that this is the end goal – to let them go. This is what it's all about.

But it is hard. The great difficulty for every mother is that you've spent all your life protecting your children from danger, guarding them, making sure that no one could ever do them harm – physical or emotional. But letting them go exposes them to all of this. I remember when our daughter Katie was eleven and went into the city centre shops on her own for the first time. Dianne and I followed her. I nearly got arrested diving in and out of shop doorways. But we can't always protect them from pain, or failure, or from some boy or girl breaking their heart. The truth is that these things are a necessary part of the very process of moving into adulthood.

We may try to control our children but ultimately we cannot do it. John White, psychiatrist and author of *Parents in Pain*, put it like this: 'You cannot control another human being, even if that human being is your own child. You do not have the right to. You may discipline and teach; you may train; you may point out the right course; you may "shape behaviour patterns"; you may reason; you may plead. But you cannot and may not ever control.'[8]

One day a woman walked in a garden. The day was wonderful and the flowers were prolific. She could smell the promise of summer in the wind. And then she saw it. At first she thought it was a dead leaf hanging on from the winter, but then she moved closer and saw it was a chrysalis. And suddenly it moved. The baby butterfly inside was trying to get out. She found it almost distressing watching its pathetic efforts and finally she could stand it no more. She rushed indoors, got a small knife, and gently prised apart the hard skin of the chrysalis so the butterfly could escape. She saw a wing emerge and then another. It was a beautiful sight; this young one emerging to adulthood. And then it tried to fly but fell to the floor. It tried again – and again. This was strange. A butterfly that couldn't even get off the ground.

Later the woman related to a friend what had happened. The friend, who knew about these things, explained: 'I'm sure you meant well, but when you stepped in to help you stopped a process that nature had designed to strengthen that insect's wings. The butterfly was meant to struggle inside the chrysalis; it was supposed to find it hard going for a while, because in the very act of fighting to get out, the wings become strong.'

I remember so many times running to sort things out for my children. I have finished off geography projects, love letters, and in later years kept irate bank managers at bay. But my children's mother has said to me time and time again, 'Rob, you must let them go – they have to learn themselves, even if it hurts a little.' She understood the principle of the butterfly.

Almost ten years ago I received a letter from a woman. Her husband had left her for somebody else and she had borne alone the responsibility of bringing up their children. I can imagine that it may be even harder for a single-parent mum to let go, but in the letter was a poem that convinced me that this mum understood what so many mothers have told me – that if you let them go you generally keep them.

> *She is gone.*
> *The child I once knew*
> *And in her place a woman.*
> *Vulnerable*
> *Lacking polish*
> *Needing assurance perhaps*
> *But nevertheless*
> *A woman.*

The pain of her birth into womanhood
Was every bit as great as the pain of her birth
The more so perhaps because of its
Suddenness.

Then there were months of waiting,
Of preparation,
Now in a day
Separation.
She's gone.

She's gone
And I must let her go.

Time now for painful rebuilding
Where innocence – now knowledge
Where wondering – now certainty
Where hesitancy – now assurance
Where once childlike trust
Now I must accept a woman's vulnerability.

View points considered – decisions made
– without me.
Ideas formulated carefully
Girlhood pushed back
– womanhood embraced
As she steps from my arms into his.

But I will wait
Not in desperation – but patiently.
For she may need me yet
As man needs man

And woman needs another woman.
And we will walk together she and I
Side by side.
For my child is gone
and in her place –
A woman.

As I finish writing this book today, I will go to visit my mother . . .

And when I do I will find that time has performed its great trick and the child has become the parent and the mother the child. Sometimes I arrive at supper-time and if so I take over the task of feeding her. I will put food on a spoon and hold it to her mouth, encouraging her to finish the plate. Then I will ask her, 'Would you like a drink?'

And when I have done that I will talk to her – oh, not talk that you would understand, she is long past that now, but rather the kind of conversation she had with me as she put me to bed when I was small. And then I will tuck the bedclothes in around her, and straighten the top sheet, bend to kiss her and say, 'Shall we say prayers?' And then a strange thing will happen: this woman who can scarcely string three words together will take my hand and in a strong voice say word-perfect the prayer she said with me each night as she put me to bed, 'Our Father, who art in heaven, hallowed be thy name . . .' And if I close my eyes I can imagine her there – all those years ago – young and pretty, and hassled, and praying for her children.

She was not a perfect mother. But she loved, and did

her best. Those two qualities elevate ordinary mothers to superhuman status, which is why children scrawl the same words on mothers' day cards the world over. I am no exception to this rule and before I leave her I always go through the same routine: 'You're the best mother in the world – did you know that?' And a smile comes to her lips, and she says, 'Who says so?' And I reply . . . 'Oh, *everybody* knows it.'

Notes

1 Anne Taylor, *Original Poems for Infant Minds* (1804).
2 James Finn Garner, *Politically Correct Bedtime Stories* (Souvenir Press Ltd, 1994).
3 Kate Saunders, quoted by Matthew and Victoria Glendinning, eds., *Sons and Mothers* (Virago Press, 1997).
4 Rob Parsons, *The Sixty Minute Father* (Hodder & Stoughton, 1995).
5 Mary Bourgoin, 'Working Mothers – Supermums or Drones' (an article published in the *Washington Post*).
6 Alice Thomas Ellis, *The Other Side of the Fire* (Penguin, 1985).
7 Erma Bombeck, *Family – The Ties that Bind . . . and Gag!* (Fawcett Books, 1998).
8 John White, *Parents in Pain* (InterVarsity Press, 1979).

Also by Rob Parsons:

The Sixty Minute Father

An Hour to Change Your Child's Life

'*A book that helps you achieve
the most important success of all.*'
SIR JOHN HARVEY-JONES

The Sixty Minute Father sets goals that can help every
father ensure that he doesn't miss out on the
greatest opportunity of his life.

- Put dates in your diary that are important for your
  children
- Talk to your baby as if she understands every word
- If you have to be away, write your child a letter
- Kneel to talk to toddlers and listen with your eyes
- Tell them how you spend your day

Full of practical advice, *The Sixty Minute Father* can be
read in about an hour but could change your
child's life forever.

Hodder & Stoughton
ISBN 0 340 63040 X

The Sixty Minute Marriage

Transform Your Relationship in One Hour

'Wise and witty. Full of down-to-earth advice that works.'
LYNDA LEE POTTER

'Sixty minutes of laughter, tears and honesty.
This life-changing book should be compulsory
reading for every couple.'
STEVE CHALKE

Following the huge success of *The Sixty Minute Father*,
Rob Parsons presents an action plan to
revolutionise every relationship.

- Are affairs good for a marriage?
- How to deal with a partner who just won't talk things through
- How to argue – effectively
- Why many men say, 'My wife's not interested in sex'
- Why cutting your credit card in half could save your marriage
- How a divorce will affect your children

Hodder & Stoughton
ISBN 0 340 67145 9